Jan. 2017

Living Literacy
at Home: A Parent's Guide
by Dr. Margaret Mary Policastro

MAUPIN HOUSE BY
CAPSTONE PROFESSIONAL
a capstone imprint

Living Literacy at Home: A Parent's Guide
By Dr. Margaret Mary Policastro

Cover Design: Peggie Carley
Interior Design: Peggie Carley

Library of Congress Cataloging-in-Publication Data
Names: Policastro, Margaret Mary.
Title: Living literacy at home: a parent's guide / Margaret Mary Policastro.
Description: North Mankato, MN : Capstone Professional, [2016] | Includes
  bibliographical references.
Identifiers: LCCN 2015044373 | ISBN 9781496606563 (pbk.) | ISBN
  9781496606570 (eBook PDF) | ISBN 9781496606587 (eBook)
Subjects: LCSH: Reading—Parent participation.
Classification: LCC LB1050.2 .P65 2016 | DDC 372.42/5--dc23
LC record available at http://lccn.loc.gov/2015044373

Image Credits:
Capstone Press: 30, 32, 44, 45, 48, 75; Dr. Margaret Mary Policastro: 10, 11, 16, 20, 28, 46, 49, 64, 67, 79, 86, 88, 95; Shutterstock: Albert Pego, 33 Top, Art Pen, Cover Design Element, Monkey Business Images, Cover, RODINA OLENA, Design Element, ThreeRivers11, 33 Bottom

Capstone Professional publishes professional resources for K–12 educators. Contact us for tailored, in-school training or to schedule an author for a workshop or conference. Visit www.capstonepd.com for free lesson plan downloads.

This book includes websites that were operating at the time it went to press.

Maupin House Publishing, Inc. by Capstone Professional
1710 Roe Crest Drive
North Mankato, MN 56003
www.capstonepd.com
888-262-6135
info@capstonepd.com

Dedication

This book is dedicated to my parents, Anne C. Piechrowski and C. Edward McMinn, who instilled the love of literacy within me. I owe all of my passion, zeal, and zest for the love of literacy to my mother. She introduced to me to books when I was very young. We went to a weekly story hour at the South Bend, Indiana, branch library, where Mrs. Krocksel, the librarian, read stories to my siblings and me. I hold those memories dear, and I'm forever grateful for the early opportunity and experiences at the library from my mother. There is no question that I was destined to be a literacy educator. And for that I am forever grateful to my parents.

I also dedicate this book to my four sons, Matthew, Timothy, Andrew, and Sebastian, who have made *Living Literacy at Home* our life. Their patience with me for allowing our lives to be a learning laboratory for literacy is forever cherished and appreciated. Every summer for 10 years, one to four of my sons would attend the Roosevelt University Summer Reading Clinic that I direct. Although it was not easy to take my children to work with me, those summers are remembered as a gift as it is where my lives as a mother and a literacy educator were truly woven into one.

Acknowledgments

I interviewed many parents for this book, asking just a few simple questions about their lives as parents and the interactions and experiences they have had at home and in school with literacy. Additionally, working in our Summer Reading Clinic at Roosevelt University, I have talked to thousands of parents over the years about their concerns, hopes, and dreams about their children's literacy development. I learned so much from all the conversations and interviews, which have informed and shaped this book. The responses are spread throughout this book, and no real names are used. I acknowledge these parents for sharing their important stories with me; parents on a quest to have lifelong literate children. During the Summer Reading Clinic of 2015, graduate students Kathleen Skinner, Rachael Buckley, Carmia Fuqua, Laurie Speicher, and Casandra Pagni and volunteers Shannon Hart, Maria Alba, Marie Aspell, Courtney Dong, and Hiral Amin were instrumental in providing parent workshops and strategies that are discussed throughout this book. I appreciate all of their contributions and ideas about how living literacy at home is something that we need to work on with parents and form a collaborative partnership around.

I also want to acknowledge Karen Soll, Managing Editor at Capstone Professional, for her unending support of my work. Karen is a dream-come-true editor who knows exactly how to move a writer forward. I also want to thank Emily Raij, also an editor for Capstone, for the feedback that shaped this book. She has a keen editing sense and knows how to move a writer forward.

This work could not happen without the support of the College of Education and the Office of Community Engagement at Roosevelt University. Dr. Thomas Phillion, Dean of the College of Education, and Dr. Teryl Rosch and Jeanne Barnas from the Office of Community Engagement provided unending support of this work. I also want to acknowledge Dr. Antonia Potenza, Associate Dean of the College of Education at Roosevelt University, who is an early childhood expert. Her knowledge about children's development and the importance of play, pretend play, and dramatic play were important in this book. She encouraged me to be sure to include all of these important topics in the book. I also want to recognize John MacDougall and Sabrina Elms in the College of Education for their assistance and guidance with the photographs for this book.

An important acknowledgement goes to the Illinois Board of Higher Education (IBHE) for supporting my work in the schools with an Improving Teacher Quality (ITQ) grant through No Child Left Behind (NCLB). This work has allowed me to collaborate in schools with teachers, school leaders, and parents in order to promote access to books for all. This access to books resulted in the development of parent libraries and family literacy nights in our schools. I would like to recognize David Wood, Principal of Our Lady of the Wayside School in Arlington Heights, Illinois; Dr. Elizabeth Alvaraz, Principal of John Dore School in Chicago, Illinois; Carolyn Jones, Principal of Perkins Bass School in Chicago; Dr. Ann Marie Riordan, Principal of Christ the King School in Chicago; Stephen Fabiyi, Principal, and Miyoshi Brown, Assistant Principal, at Metcalfe Community Academy in Chicago; and Alicia Lewis, Principal, and Dr. Pam Strauther-Sanders, Assistant Principal, of Bright School in Chicago. I also want to recognize the Roosevelt University literacy coaches Marlene Levin, Melissa Marquino-Peterson, Dr. Becky McTague, and Diane Mazeski, who all work hard to promote and maintain home and school partnerships. A special thanks goes to Jody Hunt and Dr. Dianne Gardner from IBHE.

I also want to recognize Jorie Sutton and Valerie Mercurio, student workers at Roosevelt University, for assisting in the review of the literature for this book, helping with the glossary, assisting with photographs, checking references, and much more.

Table of Contents

Foreword by Kathy Barclay

Learning to read and write are the most important skills to be developed during the early years of school, and, as author Margaret Policastro so beautifully illustrates, children who fall in love with reading when they're young are likely to enjoy it when they're older. Research indicates a strong link exists between family involvement and student benefits, such as higher academic achievement, better attendance, and improved behavior at home and school. Studies also show that parents care about their children and want to be involved in their children's education; however, they do not always know what they can or should be doing at home to support academic learning. Becoming literate is a process that begins in the first three years and continues throughout one's life. The interactions young children have with literacy materials, such as books, paper, and crayons, and with the adults in their lives are the building blocks for language, reading, and writing development. It is these building blocks of language and literacy that comprise the foundation upon which all future academic learning is built.

Ensuring a successful academic experience for all children is a monumentally important task, one that requires effective communication and collaboration among schools, families, and students. Included within *Living Literacy at Home* is a wealth of information and ideas to help parents make every day a literacy-rich day. Parents will also find helpful information about school expectations, communicating with teachers, preparing for parent-teacher conferences, and building strong home-school connections.

Home and school are the two most important institutions in a child's life; the meaningful and purposeful intersection of these serve to benefit both. This is precisely why both parents and educators need *Living Literacy at Home*. Parental involvement is a key instructional strategy that, when used appropriately, can make teaching more effective. And parental involvement in literacy-related activities outside of school has been shown to be strongly related to children's reading performance.

Readers of *Living Literacy at Home* will discover tried and true family-friendly supports for promoting the early and lasting development of critical life skills in reading, writing, listening, and speaking. Margaret Policastro draws upon her work as a literacy educator and her experiences as the parent of four boys to create this gem of a book. Aimed at bringing key aspects of home and school together to create strong lifelong readers and writers, *Living Literacy at Home* is a valuable resource for parents as well as for teachers whose goal is to provide parents with resources for supporting their children's academic success.

Kathy H. Barclay, Ed.D., Professor Emeritus,
Western Illinois University and author of
*Together We Can: Uniting Families, Schools
and Communities to Help All Children Learn,*
2nd ed. (Kendall Hunt, 2009)

Introduction

As the mother of four sons and a literacy educator, I have had the luxury of living out my passion of preparing teachers to teach children how to read. Moreover, having the experience of watching the development of my sons' reading and writing allowed me to better understand what I already knew and learned from research and theory. As a mom, I was fortunate not to have to "switch hats" from mother to literacy educator, as these roles blurred into one for me. Consequently, taking my work home with me was and is a constant joy. With my sons, everything literacy related was always done with a keen eye and sense of wonder as I watched every minute of their literacy development emerge and unfold. Since literacy was what I knew most about, it was natural for me to fill their lives and our home with a print-rich environment. Furthermore, experiences were planned and executed with a sense of how this would contribute to their overall knowledge base and get them ready for school reading.

I was always thinking about what information I could translate back to my classroom at the university to inform my students. What real-life examples could be shared as "off-the-press" emergent literacy moments were happening? Often, our experiences were not planned and happened in the moment. For example, playing in the park would be redirected many times as we captured the essence of a butterfly, a frog, or dark clouds rolling in before a summer storm. Memories were made, but more important, we captured the moments with conversations, documentation, and wonder questions that allowed us to pursue many trips to the public library to look for more information. We took a lot of time to think about nature, wonders, and all the things that little minds bring forth. I became a better literacy educator, utilizing examples, artifacts, models, and real-life stories from my children. In our family, we marveled and celebrated firsthand every moment of our daily adventures, which were rich in language. What is and appears to look like "children playing" actually becomes some of the most important experiences

that shape and inform language and literacy development. Watching a butterfly, a frog, or the clouds in the sky always provided a time for wonderment, inquiry, and conversation. One spring, after planting an apple tree in the backyard with meticulous care in the planning, our son asked "OK, now when are we going to put the apples on?" His grandfather and I just looked at each other and had no immediate response. On an early July evening, just as the lightning bugs began to flutter, our son asked "How do they turn on and off their headlights?" Once again, I had no immediate response but said that was an interesting question and we definitely needed to look for the answer. Often, an interest would begin to develop from these experiences, which would connect to a book or other print sources.

Over time, print and nonprint information accumulated in our home on topics, such as frogs, dinosaurs, building bridges, and much more. A "butterfly sighting" sheet was posted near the back door so the children could record their findings. Playing in the sand or flying model airplanes led to discussions enriching the experience. Each experience was a moment to witness the children's language, thinking, problem-solving, and vocabulary unfold. There is no question that the amount of parent-child language interaction and exposure to print in the home impacts the school learning environment and success (Carter, Chard & Pool, 2009).

While observing a kindergarten class, I watched the morning routine of calendar time unfold. The teacher asked the children what day it was, and when they discussed it was the first day of February, one student asked, "What happened to January? Where did it go?" These questions form an important part of children's thinking and language development, which are critical to literacy. These types of questions and inquiry also lead to thoughtful conversations and interactions with text and non-text information, expanding vocabulary and more. According to Craig-Post (2015), "research indicates richness of vocabulary is the major predictor of good reading skills." Thus, activities that promote language, conversation, and vocabulary development are all critical to reading.

When children ask questions about the world and specifically things they don't know and want to know about, it is a sign that they are monitoring their learning. Not knowing about something but having the yearning to know it or know more is essential to lifelong learning. As parents, we need to be on the lookout for such instances and capitalize on the moment. Research shows that children who self-monitor their learning—that is, know when they know, don't know, or need further help—are strategic learners. I remember seeing my son self-monitor when he was in preschool and I bought modeling clay for him. I set it up on the kitchen counter and had him all ready to go when he announced to me, "Mommy, I don't know clay. I don't know what to do with it." I remember thinking how silly it was of me to introduce him to something new and expect him to "know" what it is about and how to use it. Important here is that he knew he didn't know, and he expressed it to me. Some children, as they are developing in their learning, don't know if they know and don't know if they don't know. Parents need to model for their children when they don't know something. Some examples might be:

- "I don't know too much about grasshoppers and would like to learn more."

- "I wonder why a giraffe has such a long neck. I would like to learn more about that."

- "I don't know where the country of _____ is and would like to find out."

What does it mean to live literacy at home? This question is one we need to face as parents. Literacy is essential to survival in our print-rich and ever-changing digital society. As parents we need to stand strong and align to the challenges that face public education today. We must be willing and ready to partner with schools and teachers to ensure our children get the best, top-quality instruction in literacy. This is a two-way street and it can't all be placed in the school or all in the home. There must be a mutual collaboration that bears the richness of a literate future for all of our children.

This book grew out of the many years of parenting and working with parents in our Summer Reading Clinic at Roosevelt University. This clinic is the practicum experience for teachers who are in training to become reading specialists. In essence, this is like a small **balanced literacy** school where children from the community come to be engaged in literacy over the summer. "Balanced literacy" is a philosophical orientation that assumes reading and writing achievement are developed through instruction and support in multiple environments in which teachers use various approaches that differ by level of teacher support and child control (Frey, et al 2005; Fountas & Pinnell, 1996). This perspective espouses that there is not one right approach to teaching reading (Fitzgerald, 1999), but rather a balanced approach to literacy development, involving decision-making through which the teacher makes thoughtful choices about the best way for students to become successful readers and writers (Spiegel, 1998).

Over the years, we have seen a consistent set of concerns from parents at the clinic:

- "We are both engineers and know nothing about how to help our two children with reading and writing. We were not into reading, still are not avid readers, and don't know where to begin."

- "My third-grade daughter doesn't like to write, and her spelling and grammar are very weak. I have tried to help her, but I just don't know how."

- "My son has no interest in reading, and I don't think that he has ever read a book from start to finish."

- "My second-grade daughter is behind in reading, and I don't know how to help her. I don't want her to fall further behind in school."

- "My fifth-grade son knows how to read but doesn't want to read. He only wants to play video games. Getting homework done is always a challenge."

One important idea that I have gleaned from my years of working in schools and in our clinic with parents is that parents are indeed both an important and necessary resource for helping their children with language and literacy development. Reese, Sparks, and Leyva (2010) state, "Parents are an untapped resource for improving children's language and literacy." Although their work centered on young children and families, I believe that parents are indeed an untapped resource throughout the school years. About 10 years ago, we started offering parent workshops in the morning from 8:30 to 9:00 a.m., before the clinic session began. We were overwhelmed by the participation. At first, the workshops were just for parents, and then we started having interactive, hands-on workshops where the parents could learn and try out an activity with their children. These workshops provided information to parents on all aspects of literacy (much of what is presented in this book). What has been collected from this work is the following:

- Parents want to know how their children are progressing in both reading and writing.

- Parents want real-time feedback about their children's literacy development.

- Parents want support and specific recommendations in all aspects of literacy development at home, including fun activities.

- Parents want and seek out information about parenting and literacy development.

- Parents want to know how to participate in home-school partnerships and have strong communication with teachers.

The purpose of this book is to provide information to parents, grandparents, and caregivers, so they can better understand how their children are progressing in literacy development in school and at home. The activities in this book utilize free daily literacy experiences that are all around us. The point is that living literacy at home does not need to cost a lot of money. Rather, caregivers can take advantage of the life that surrounds us. Moreover, the intention is for parents, grandparents, and caregivers to forge good home-school partnerships. Most importantly, this book will teach others how to live literacy daily and learn and grow as a parent.

This book is designed to get you going, no matter where you might be in your quest to living literacy at home, with an abundance of easy-to-implement activities, tips, and routines. The field of education is full of technical vocabulary that is used by teachers and school administrators, so there is a glossary beginning on page 109 that defines each term bolded in black throughout the book and some additional terms. Online Literacy Resources are listed on page 107, too, offering suggestions for further reading and literacy activities.

For some, these ideas will not be new, but rather an integration of what you are already doing. Others might find the ideas and concepts to be completely new. Either way, the information is presented for you to develop your own unique way to live literacy at home. There is no one formula; rather, you select ideas that work for your specific situation and family. The intention is not to make your home into a "mini-school" where your child feels like he or she is back in class. The intention is to experience life through the lens of literacy every day. You are probably already doing much of what is in this book. My hope is that you gain some fresh strategies and a new awareness of how to make literacy come alive for your family on a daily basis.

Chapter One: The State of Literacy in School

What Children Need to Know When Entering School

There is a great sense of urgency in today's classrooms. The urgency is centered on teaching children to read and write as demands from districts continue to grow. A recent U.S. government publication titled *The Nation's Report Card* stated that when students do not read well, they are more likely to be retained in school, drop out of high school, become a teen parent, or enter the juvenile system. Kotaman (2013) states, "Students who are the poorest readers in the early years of primary school tend to remain poor readers for the rest of their academic lives." Indeed, teachers and administrators feel this enormous sense of urgency for students to achieve and perform well. What does this sense of urgency look like? Recently, I visited a first-grade classroom where the children were gathered on the carpet reciting **vocabulary** words. The teacher would say a word, and the children would repeat it, define it, and discuss it. Some of the words were "hurricane," "rigorous," and "computer." In another class, the second-grade teacher was assessing children in small guided reading groups. The kindergarten teacher was showing the children how to count by 10s, which required reading the directions as the lesson unfolded. The other first-grade class was busy getting ready for a vocabulary assessment. An eighth-grade class had just finished *To Kill a Mockingbird* and were taking an open-book assessment. Carter, Chard & Pool (2009) state, "Despite the importance of language and literacy development, however, more than one-third of children in the United States enter school with significant differences in language, early literacy skills, and motivation to learn that place them at considerable risk for developing long-term reading difficulties." Imagine the challenge this presents for teachers.

What Literacy Is and the Influence of Technology

Your definition of **literacy** and family literacy will change and grow as you go through this book. Living literacy at home is an ever-changing process, and hopefully one that you will see as a lifelong journey. When we think of the word "literacy," most people associate it with reading printed materials. However, the term has a broader definition. "The most common understanding of literacy is that it is a set of tangible skills—particularly the cognitive skills of reading and writing" (UNESCO, 2006). However, literacy is a complex term and includes other important factors. For example, life experiences are critical to the development of literacy in that readers and writers depend on their knowledge base of the world as they read and write. When readers read about a topic, such as trains, all the information they have stored in their brain will help in the comprehension of the material. This will include both print and nonprint information, such as pictures of trains, videos about trains, conversations about trains, and more. What contributes to this experience is the reader's personal experience with trains. Perhaps riding the train is an important part of the life of the student. Barone (2015) states, "there is no one fixed definition of literacy; rather literacy is redefined every day." She explains that literacy includes foundational skills that are changing in terms of how children learn letters—not just from print sources, but with technology. Contributing to the changing definition is **multimodal literacy,** or multiple forms of making meaning and communicating.

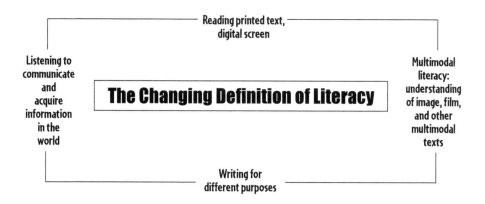

There is no question that technology has influenced literacy in the home, at school, and throughout the world. Cohen and Cowen (2011) state, "Electronic forms of communication, such as e-mail, text messaging, social networking, and blogs, are drastically altering our concept of literacy and how we communicate with others. It is the Internet, however, that has brought unprecedented changes to the way in which people spend their time and access information." Technology in the home has changed the way families function, communicate, and live out their daily lives. Young children now have access to electronic devices that introduce them to sounds, letters, words, stories, and much more. Their knowledge about the world is constantly increasing as they interact with computers, having access to any and all topics. Games and entertainment devices are full of text that no doubt engages the user. Through all of these interactions and encounters with technology, children have access to print like never before in our history. Technology has also caused a transformation in pedagogy and delivery of lessons within schools. Classrooms now have computers and other devices to help students in all aspects of their language and literacy development. With Google at their fingertips, parents and children can inquire about any topic of interest.

> **The International Society for Technology in Education (ISTE) is a worldwide nonprofit organization promoting technology education in schools.**

The world is a different place because of technology. In our global world, our children will need to be technology savvy in order to be successful. As parents, we need to develop ways in which the use of technology works in our family. Each family will be different in implementing and utilizing technology to meet ever-changing family needs. Although technology is an important dimension with all of the interactive books and educational tools available, it is not a replacement for the wonderful bonding activity of reading to and with your child every day. Therefore:

- Evaluate the family needs for all technology in the home.

- Set limits on use and accessibility based on your family needs.

- Utilize technology for reading, writing, inquiry, research, and communication.

- Check out talking books.

- Encourage communication through e-mail, texting, blogs, and other sources.

- Try out speech-to-text technology.

- Use social media as appropriate for your family's needs.

- Go on a virtual field trip. (See tips in the Appendix.)

Why Talking to Your Child Is Important

Children learn words and language from the world around them. One important dimension to this is the conversations they have with parents and others. Talk is an important aspect in the development of language and literacy skills for children. Talking requires thinking or cognitive skills in order to say something or respond to someone. In order to talk, you must retrieve words and thoughts from your memory and express them in speech. Listening during conversations requires that you to store the information being processed. As we talk and listen, we are constantly thinking about how to respond.

Powell and D'Angelo (2000) state, "since the 1950s, researchers have found that a range of parenting beliefs and behaviors are positively associated with children's literacy and school-related outcomes." They outline both direct and indirect behaviors that contribute to literacy development. The primary direct way is to have engaging, "language-rich verbal exchanges." Indirect behaviors include providing reading and writing materials and serving as role models in everyday life. As children listen and respond to language and think about what they are hearing, they are constantly constructing new meaning. This new meaning is derived from all of their background knowledge and experiences. Starting with young children and making an effort to have engaging daily conversations will enrich their lives as they get older. Teens especially need to be engaged and included in family discourse as they are seeking answers and making meaning out of their lives.

Listening → Thinking → Talking

Constructing New Meaning

What Does Literacy Instruction Look Like in Today's Classroom?

It is important for parents to have an understanding of and a glimpse into classroom literacy instruction today. What does the literacy environment look like in today's classroom? What is expected of children when they enter school? In elementary schools, there is typically a block of time set aside each day for literacy instruction. This is often referred to as the **literacy block** or routine.

This block of time ranges from 90 to 180 minutes or more. Within this time frame, teachers cover an enormous amount of learning material generally aligned with the standards for language arts. A typical literacy block of instruction might contain the elements listed on page 21. Descriptions of some elements follow.

Typical Literacy Block Routine

- **Read-aloud** (15 minutes)
- **Journal time** (15 minutes)
- **Whole group instruction** (15–20 minutes)
- **Small group guided reading** (20-minute rotation)
- **Small group center time** (20-minute rotation)
- **Independent reading and writing** (20-minute rotation)

Read-aloud

In many elementary school classrooms, the day begins with a **read-aloud** of text that is read to the children by the teacher. The read-aloud is usually aligned to a literacy standard and has a purpose for the lesson. The children usually gather together and sit in front of the teacher on a carpet. The teacher will begin reading either a fiction or nonfiction selection, stop at key points, and ask the children questions. An **interactive read-aloud** allows the children to respond to questions on individual whiteboards and then share and discuss their answers. Young children might have the option to respond in print or to draw a picture. This requires the children to listen attentively to the information. Children who have been read to at home before entering school find this to be a natural extension from home to school. To promote a smooth transition from home to school:

- Read-aloud daily, and include fiction and nonfiction books.
- For older children and teens, read novels and **informational text** as a family, and have "family book clubs" and discussions.
- Point out the author and illustrator when reading and looking at books.
- Talk about the book cover.
- Talk about the illustrations on the cover and in the book.
- Ask prediction types of questions, such as "Look at the picture. What do you think is going to happen next?"
- Check the public library for story hours and author visits.
- Discuss and have conversations about the books read.
- Talk about an interesting word.
- Keep a list of books read.

Journal Time

Many classrooms have opportunities for children to write in a journal. Ongoing writing activities become an important part of the literacy routine. Teachers might provide a prompt for children to respond to or allow children to write about topics on their own. Generating written text is an important goal of this activity. Often, when this activity is started in the early grades, it becomes a natural part of the school experience. In primary grades, journaling is used by teachers to promote **emergent literacy** development. For some children, expressing their thoughts on paper is not an easy task. Getting young children to generate thoughts in writing or through dictation early on is an important step to writing. To encourage writing at home:

- Keep a journal and model the writing process for your child.

- Encourage your child to keep a journal and write daily.

- Don't focus on correcting young children's spelling as they are working toward the development of their spelling skills.

- Write lists together (e.g., grocery, tasks to accomplish, etc.).

- Leave notes to your child, and ask open-ended questions, such as "What did you read and discuss at school today?"

Small Group Guided Reading Instruction

Many classrooms work with students in small groups to provide **guided reading** instruction. During guided reading, the teacher works with a small group of five to seven children who have similar reading behaviors. The teacher matches the text to the children's reading level. Guided reading provides a special time for the teacher to interact with each student, monitoring reading behaviors while providing feedback to move the student forward.

Independent Reading and Writing

Most classrooms today have time for children to read and write independently. During this time, children have the opportunity to select books from the **classroom library** and read silently for an uninterrupted period of time. Often, this is considered recreational reading, or the teacher might have a specific purpose for the independent reading that aligns with a classroom lesson or theme. For example, if the class is studying a particular topic related to bugs, the children might have an opportunity to read more about bugs on their own. Independent writing can function in the same manner whereby the writing time could have a specific purpose related to the topic. This kind of instruction requires that the student work for a period of time independently. For some children, settling down into a book to read or a topic to write about requires discipline and structure. Children who enjoy reading and writing tend to do well during this independent time. To help children adapt well to **independent reading and writing** time at school, you can do the following at home:

- Model reading and writing at home daily.
- Schedule quiet time (turn off the television) for recreational reading and writing.
- Plan trips to the library, allow your child to select books of interest, and stay at the library to read in a quiet spot.
- Have your child keep a journal and write daily.
- Set up a home library, and add to the collection. Include both fiction and nonfiction sources.
- For older children and teens, set up routines for independent reading and writing time, and read young adult novels with your child.

Research shows that reading aloud is the single most important thing you can do to help a child prepare for learning. Reading 15 minutes every day for five years (the time before kindergarten) adds up to more than 456 hours and makes a huge difference, according to Read Aloud, an organization committed to spreading the word about the importance of reading. Read Aloud also notes that more than 15 percent of young children (3.1 million) are read to by family members fewer than three times a week. The benefits of reading aloud to your child include enhancing language development, encouraging all literacy skills, brain development, and instilling a love of reading.

High-stakes Assessments and Common Core State Standards

Schools today are mandated to execute **high-stakes assessments.** These national assessments are required by law, and each state determines which assessments will be given to the students. High-stakes assessments promote a culture of testing within schools that puts pressure on teachers, administrators, and children to perform. Often, teachers spend a great deal of time preparing students to take these exams. Within schools, the test is generally perceived as consequential to the school and/or district. Consequences for students may include not getting a diploma or moving to the next grade. For teachers, it could be that their performance is based in part on how well their students do on such tests. For schools, it could mean the future of the school is in jeopardy—even resulting in school closure. Most often, there is a focus on "getting test ready" in the community for both the tests and the results (Policastro, McTague & Mazeski, 2016). With the new **Common Core State Standards** (CCSS), states are required to provide assessments, such as the Partnership for Assessment of Readiness for College and Careers (PARCC) and the Smarter Balanced Assessments, to measure whether students are mastering the standards. The frequency of administering these high-stakes assessments adds to the pressure schools are under to perform. The administration in some districts can be as frequent as every other month. This often means that in between the test administrations, there is a great deal of time spent on the preparation to take the assessments. The Northwest Evaluation Association (NWEA) developed the Measures of Academic Progress (MAP) assessments, which are administered three to four times a year in many districts. This is a computerized assessment and reports results on individual children. The National Assessment of Educational Progress (NAEP) yields data as a national representation and does not report scores for individual students or schools. In December 2015, the Elementary and Secondary Education Act (ESEA) was reauthorized and replaces the No Child Left Behind (NCLB) law. The new ESEA will still require mandatory testing between grades 3 and 8 but according to Moser (2015), "The new ESEA gives the power back to the states deciding which tests to administer." A typical school calendar for assessments in one large urban district might look like this:

Grades K–2	
NWEA MAP Assessments	September/October January May

Grades 3–8	
NWEA MAP Assessments	September/October January May
PARCC Assessment	March May

Grade K–12	
State Testing	January March
NAEP (U.S. Department of Education)	January

Clearly, from the above calendar, assessment is on the minds of school leaders, teachers, and students during many months of the academic school year.

The CCSS were initiated by governors and state commissioners of education in the United States. This initiative had the goal of developing a set of shared standards and, according to Kendall (2011), "ensuring that students in every state are held to the same level of expectations that students in the world's highest-performing countries are, and that they gain the knowledge and skills that will prepare them for success in postsecondary education and the global arena." The CCSS have set learning expectations by grade for English language arts and mathematics. With these standards come shifts in thinking about instruction. The shifts are listed on the next page.

Instructional Shifts That Influence Classrooms and Home Literacy

Shift	Classroom	Home
Increase the use of informational and complex text	Students interact and engage with 50 percent more informational and complex text.	Provide informational text sources for your child, such as newspapers, magazines, and books about the world.
Find evidence from text	Students are required to find text-based answers to questions.	During discussions and reading, ask your child to point to/seek out evidence in texts (see Finding the Evidence Game on page 113 of the Appendix).
Build argumentation skills	Students develop habits of building evidentiary arguments through classroom discourse.	Pose questions in which your child will need to produce evidence to make an argument and a point.
Develop persuasion and debate skills	Students learn the skills of persuasion and developing arguments and evidence for debates.	Read the newspaper with your child, and select issues that work for debates.

Here are some other things you can do at home to focus on learning, not just the assessment:

- Keep the culture of high-stakes assessment that is in the schools out of your home.

- Communicate with school leaders and teachers about the formal assessments that schools administer.

- Explain to your children that tests are just one measure of their learning progress.

- If you are unsure about what the assessments are measuring or the results that your child receives, don't hesitate to request a conference with your child's teacher.

Chapter Two: Making Every Day a Literacy-rich Day

Making every day a literacy-rich day should not feel like a burden or add extra pressure and stress to your already busy life. In fact, the intent is to show ways in which you are already living literacy at home. As we go about our normal daily routines and activities, we are constantly interacting with print, information, and language on many levels. This chapter brings to life some of the literacy encounters we have that can be shared with children to enhance their learning. Eliciting conversations that feel natural and authentic are important. Do what feels comfortable for you and your child.

The Joy of Reading

One of the goals I had for each of my sons was to make sure they came into contact with lots of books with the hopes of developing the love and joy of reading. Trips to the public library and bookstores were something that happened often. In order to develop lifelong readers and writers, the experiences must be joyful. Promoting the joy of reading is a gift that parents can pass on to their children.

My joy of reading evolved from my lifelong experiences at public libraries. Libraries have always been an important part of my personal life: a place for retreat, comfort, knowledge, culture, and enjoyment. As I reflect on my earliest literacy experiences, I remember weekly trips with my mother and younger siblings to story hours at the public library. The library provided an inspiring space for homework in elementary school, with leisurely walking breaks through the stacks to see what I might read next. Summer afternoons were filled with time to work toward the summer reading program certificate of completion that would be displayed in the library window for the local community to view. High school pulled me in deeper with teen magazines, homework, and research. My indulgence continued throughout college when my work-study job landed me in the Indiana University library's government publications section to shelve books and work at the reference desk. I read all of the U.S. Department of Education's publications on reading that were available. Libraries have always nurtured my soul, inspired me, and provided a happy place I could count on. My dedication to libraries must be in my blood. Thus, as a parent, I couldn't wait to take my children to the public library for story hours, to check out books, and to experience the other events and activities the library offered. Passing on this love was important to me.

Similarly, bookstores were a place for developing the joy of reading. One cold January evening, Gary Paulsen, author of *Hatchet*, was in town to promote a new book. All four of my sons attended this event. Each of them stood in line waiting for an autograph. This was a life-changing event for them. A brief encounter with and autograph from a famous baseball player who wrote his memoir is a bookstore memory my children still talk about today. Here are a few places you can look into:

- Special programs, such as story hours, for young children.
- Programming and after-school activities for teens.
- Community calendars announcing plays, movies, and theater events.
- Author visits and book signings.

Activities to Promote and Celebrate Literacy

Activities to promote and celebrate literacy each day are indeed all around us and in our homes. The kitchen is a great place to enhance family literacy as the space draws us together for meals, snacks, conversations, food preparation, and much more. Meals are the perfect time to have conversations about the day. Planning meals together is a great way to introduce interesting words to your child. Looking

at cookbooks and letting your child plan a meal encourages creativity and interaction with a specific kind of food language. The kitchen is also a place to promote healthy eating, which can bring in additional literacy activities. Kids can do research on organic vs. nonorganic foods, the effects of consuming too much sugar, and other inquiry topics. Getting your child to read and think critically to make informed decisions is an important life skill, and the kitchen offers numerous opportunities. Here are some things you can do:

- Keep a bulletin board in the kitchen to post family activities, a calendar of events, weekly menus, and other important family dates or notes.

- Find a space (wall or cabinet door) to highlight food vocabulary—appetizer, sandwich, jalapeño, balsamic, zucchini, polenta, cantaloupe, marshmallow— and have fun talking about these words and using them in your conversations and meal planning.

- Plan holiday meals and other meal celebrations with your child. Have lots of conversations about what goes into the planning of the meal and what is needed.

- Make grocery and planning lists with your child. Post them in the kitchen.

- Post menus and recipes, and discuss them with your child. Let your child develop and create meals.

- Keep a chore list in the kitchen to show how all family members contribute. Have your child participate in the making of the list.

- For fun, keep a box or basket of pots and pans and other kitchen utensils for your young child to play with. Encouraging play with household kitchen items will elicit conversation, pretend play, and interest in cooking.

In the Kitchen

For Younger Children:

- Food and product labels: Help children recognize environmental print around them and realize they have meaning.

- Grocery lists: Model writing shopping lists and share them with your child; cut out food pictures and logos from advertisements or food labels, and have your child create a grocery list using the pictures and labels.

- Playing with print: Use store ads for different sorting activities, such as cutting out words and pictures to be sorted into baskets or bowls by type of items.

- Recipes and cookbooks: Use print and pictures in cookbooks and recipes to start vocabulary discussions.

For Older Children:

- Have your child find a recipe and read it to you as you cook.

- Have your child put the ingredients in the correct sequence of use.

- Have your child measure the ingredients.

- Have your child plan meals, find recipes, and research nutrition and health benefits of foods.

Neighborhoods are flooded with **environmental print** that most of us don't pay attention to. We recognize it and know its function but don't do much to celebrate the language all around us. Print messages in the community provide ample opportunities to have fun and interesting conversations while in the car or on foot. Keep the conversations lighthearted, but use them as a springboard for discussion and learning. In the neighborhood there are great print and nonprint sources to pay attention to: street names, building names, advertisements, billboards, posted signs, bus stops, and route signs, etc. Road signs can elicit wonderful conversations about what all those symbols mean. Look for patterns in street names (trees: Olive, Locust, Maple, Oak; presidents: Adams, Washington, Monroe, Madison). Look up the difference between a street, avenue, lane, road, trail, and boulevard. Look up the history of the origin of a street's name. And don't overlook those construction sites as they have lots of offer. Stopping to watch a construction site in action can be an on-the-spot learning encounter for the whole family and can build upon interests your children may already have in machines, trucks, or building. Informational text can be followed up with your child about street signs, buildings, bridges, construction cranes, concrete, steel, lumber, wood, bricks, electricians, masons, carpenters, and job-site safety.

Architecture is another way to evoke interesting conversations with your child. Houses, churches, temples, commercial buildings, and even bridges all have certain attributes and characteristics that can bring forth abundant conversation. Point out ornate and plain details on a building, or discuss the year a building was built and how that affected its style. This all adds to your child's ongoing development of knowledge and information.

Restaurants provide interesting topics for discussion. Talk about the difference between a fast food restaurant and more formal dining. Specialty restaurants that focus on ethnic foods can bring about discussions of cultures and foods from around the world. There are so many different kinds of restaurants that cover a variety of cultures, such as Mediterranean, French, Italian, Greek, and more. Collect menus from different restaurants, and research the different foods that each offers. Research the culture and background of the countries that the food represents. While in a restaurant, talk to your child about all the print information that fills the setting. Use the five senses to notice the way the restaurant is decorated, the service, the way the foods smell and feel, and the different tastes. Encourage your child to participate in as much restaurant reading as possible. Point to the letters and words on the menu. Teach your child new words as you explore different types of foods. Write a mock review for the restaurant.

Environmental print provides families a way to encourage reading in a fun, natural way. We are bombarded with a variety of print while traveling in a car, bus, taxi, train, boat, or plane. Take time on these trips to point out interesting words and pictures on billboards, restaurants, signs, license plates, and safety or warning signs. School-age children are not too young to discuss bike and pedestrian safety. Ask what they think certain signs or symbols mean, and see if they know the definitions of words like "yield." Try not to give away the answers. Let children look and think first, or help them find the answer together from print and nonprint sources. For older children and teens, signs on the road prepare them for driving a vehicle, getting around a city, and being a good citizen.

I remember when one of my sons was in kindergarten and asked to go to the restroom while we were at a fast food restaurant. We were sitting just a few feet away, so I watched him head toward the restrooms. He looked up to the left and then up to the right, came back to me, and said "Mom, I can't find the one that says 'Kids.'" I love this example, as it highlights how children are reading all the signs within their environment and making meaning of their world. Moreover, in this example, my son was looking for signs that represented age, not just gender, so he was bringing different topics into his little study of environmental print.

While visiting a first-grade class, I heard the teacher ask the children if Ruby Bridges was alive today, and the children did not know. The teacher then said, "What do we do if we don't know something?" and all the children in unison said "We Google it." When you are with your child and a question is posed, don't simply give answers. Use this as an opportunity for inquiry and to go into more depth or research on a topic. Going from nonprint to print to digital and other modes makes getting the answer more interesting and fun. Use these moments as opportunities for your child to let you know that he or she does not know something. You also can model this by saying, "I am not familiar with this, but I would like to learn more about it." Adults have lots to learn, too!

Conversation Ideas: Parent Talk

- "I wonder how clouds are made."
- "I wonder why some flowers have a scent."
- "I wonder who invented the bicycle and also how long it has been around."
- "I wonder where coffee beans come from."
- "I wonder why the price of gasoline is cheaper today than last year."
- "I wonder when it will rain again."

For older children and teens, challenge them and ask questions that go beyond their current knowledge base. Require them to seek and find new information:

- "I wonder what we can do as a family to help support this cause."
- "I wonder about this environmental issue and the effects it is having on the world."
- "I wonder what inspired this artist/musician to create this work."

Be a Role Model: Spend Time Reading, Writing, Talking, and Listening

Both my mother and my sister were avid readers when I was growing up. My mother would check out thick books from the public library to read. My older sister was a voracious reader and plowed through book after book. She read all of the Nancy Drew books. I wanted to be like my sister and sustain long periods of silent reading. She could spend an entire Saturday afternoon reading the same book. My mother and father both read the local newspaper from front to back. We subscribed to *Reader's Digest*, which was always available to read. My mother also received a Polish newspaper, which she looked forward to reading. I looked at the pictures and wondered what the articles were about, trying to read Polish. All of these early experiences modeled the importance of reading. My mother took pride in her handwriting and used to make long, specific grocery lists. I would then have to go to the local grocer and get groceries from the list. I remember learning about "distilled water" and the other interesting terms on her lists.

My mother did not graduate from high school as she had to leave during her sophomore year to take care of her sister who was ill. Despite this lack of formal education, my mother served as a stellar literacy role model for me. In fact, her love of literacy was passed on to me. Memories abound as I reflect back on sitting in the kitchen and asking my mother about the *Diary of Anne Frank* and the Lindbergh kidnapping. I was deeply interested in reading about both of these topics, and my mother could tell me details of what she remembered from living through those times. She indulged me with her own background knowledge in conversations we often shared. These memories are priceless to me.

My mother and father were very involved in Bluebirds, Camp Fire, Cub Scouts, and Boy Scouts. Weekly meetings at our house turned the dining room table into a headquarters where scouts were busy doing all sorts of activities. My younger brother's love of scouting, camping, recreation, and the outdoors proved to be his lifelong passion. Today he is an administrator for the parks and recreation department in our hometown. I use this as an example of how important modeling and encouraging personal interests are. We never know what will spark motivation for continued lifelong work.

Be literacy role models at home by showing your love of reading and creating reading spaces and an environment rich in print:

- Let your child see you reading and writing at home often.
- Make a special effort to talk to your child about the purposes of your reading and writing. ("I'm reading the newspaper to find out ..." or "I'm looking up a recipe for ..." or "I'm writing a letter to ....")
- Stress the importance of literacy in daily life activities (e.g., banking, driving, shopping, paying bills, etc.).
- Talk about the books you are reading with your child.
- Talk about reviews of books that you hope to read, sending a message that this is a continuous process and you're always interested in reading more.
- Have lots and lots of conversation within your family.

Out and About

Whether on short trips, long trips, or a family vacation, use the time out and about to grasp the literacy-rich world that exists all around us. A trip to the gas station can prompt a discussion of gas prices and how they fluctuate—a great way for older children to understand the reasons gas prices change. Stopping for that morning cup of coffee or tea can bring about the topic of where coffee and tea come from and much more. Older children can research the coffee bean and tea ingredients. The grocery store is also abundant with literacy-rich experiences. The stores' organized layout, sections, and huge variety of choices can help children go from broad to more specific concepts. For example, the produce section can be the perfect opportunity to learn about fruits and vegetables. Think of all the colors, smells, and tastes in the produce section. Conversations might also include who in the family enjoys the foods, what you are out of, and how much is needed until the next trip. Buying drinking water can be a conversation as you think and observe aloud with your child. There is bottled water that comes in plastic and glass, canned water, flavored water, carbonated water, and plain water. Grocery stores, like restaurants, also offer an opportunity to discuss ethnic foods and different cultures. One mother I interviewed told me that the grocery store is a place where she has constant conversations with her daughter. When shopping in the produce section for peppers, she discusses the difference in colors, which family members like them, and how many they should purchase. This mother used the grocery store as a learning opportunity to have conversations about the items in the store and much more.

Use the car as a literacy hot spot. Keep a bag of reading materials inside, and refresh the supply often. While in the car, sing songs, tell stories, and play games. Point out the different makes and models of cars; look for the various logos and signs; and discuss different colors, sizes, and shapes. Point out the different license plates, and see how many different states your child can locate from the plates. Have fun with bumper stickers and billboards as you drive. Here are a few more tips for bringing literacy into your everyday trips:

- While grocery shopping, stop and point to the words on the packaging.
- Point to the ingredients on a label, and show your child what is in the product.
- Discuss choices and prices with older children.
- In the car, look for interesting or unknown words on billboards and road signs.

Traveling through airports and on airplanes provides another rich venue to explore the world. Airports have information about travel routes, destinations, and more. Use this as an opportunity to learn the geography of the world. Explore the flight patterns and distances to destinations. Discover new cities and countries as you walk through the terminal together. Aviation may be a topic your child wants to investigate further, from the history of flight to the different types of planes.

Seasons and nature walks let you explore literacy outdoors. The fall is a great time to collect leaves and identify them by tree name. I have many great memories of doing this while growing up and also with my own children. Leaves can be saved and preserved by pressing them in books and ironing them between wax paper. These make nice bookmarks as well. Spring is a time to observe signs of new plant or flower growth. Planting seeds is a nice way to help children anticipate and predict at the nonprint level. Ask "what do you think will happen next?" and read books on plants and flowers to enhance the important skill of prediction. Winter walks turn into a magical wonderland when snow appears. Investigating how a snowflake or icicle is formed adds important information to a child's background knowledge. Summertime is perfect for spending hours outside observing the clouds in the sky, birds, insects, sandy beaches, and more. Oceans, lakes, rivers, and even small streams let your children observe fish, ducks, and other creatures. Discuss and research the life cycle from a tadpole to a frog, or learn how shells form. Here are a few more ideas from nature:

- While out on nature walks, take photographs of the same place, object, or scene over time and compare the changes. These photos are a way to document changes in seasons.

- Check out clouds, take pictures, and label the type, such as cirrus, cirrocumulus, cirrostratus, altostratus, and others. Study cloud formation, fog, and other aspects.

- Make a book out of the photographs, and write about the nature walk. Add artwork to the book along with pressed flowers and leaves.

- Make a rubbing of tree bark, and identify and label the tree on the rubbing. Make it into a book.

- Use white colored pencils and black construction paper to draw a picture of a winter wonderland. This is great for capturing trees after a snowfall. Write a story to go along with the pictures.

- Build a bird feeder with your child, and place it where you can observe it all year round. Pay attention to the feeder with your child and keep track of the birds that come. This is a nice way to study different kinds of birds.

- For older children and teens, encourage ways in which they can be involved in nature, sustainability, and the environment, such as getting involved in community and neighborhood events.

- As a family, talk about how you appreciate all that nature has to offer on a daily basis. Discuss your favorite parts of your favorite seasons.

Take your nature walks a step further and start a collection:

- Collect rocks and study the patterns, textures, colors, and sizes. Research the different types of rocks in your geographic area.

- Collect seashells and describe the colors, shapes, and locations where they were found.

- Collect leaves and make a leaf collage, labeling the different types of leaves.

Having fun with seasonal words can be as easy as posting them to a bulletin board in the kitchen and having conversations about them. Other easy activities include watching The Weather Channel or local weather reports and tracking weather patterns both in the newspaper and on the computer. Finding print and other digital sources to look up the words helps build vocabulary and your child's knowledge base.

Fall Words and Concepts	Winter Words and Concepts
Acorn, Cornucopia, Harvest, Leaves, Trees	Blizzard, Freezing/Frost, Ice, Snow, Temperature
Spring Words and Concepts	Summer Words and Concepts
Rain, Life cycle, Sprout, Storm, Tornado	Draught, Cumulus clouds, Heat wave, Hurricane, Ocean currents

If your family is looking to go on more than a walk, plan a family field trip. One of the best parts of a family outing is the planning that can go into it. Get children excited by letting them take the reins on the planning. Use a map to plot out the travel route while teaching map-reading skills like direction and scale.

Possible Family Field Trips

- Arboretum
- Camping
- Zoo
- Bird sanctuary
- Hiking
- Dunes
- Library
- Circus
- Family reunion
- Museum
- Bike path/tour
- County fair
- Nature center
- Forest preserve
- Ocean, lake, pond, or river

A mother of two middle-school children told me all about their recent family vacation to Texas. I asked how the destination was selected, and she said that after her daughter had done a research paper on Texas in school, she really wanted to visit the state. They ended up staying on a horse ranch and experiencing the life of a rancher firsthand. This is a great example of connecting home and school.

Reading and Writing Time Each Day

This book is all about finding ways to celebrate literacy each day. Inherent in that is reading and writing each day. Some fun ways to start writing can be as easy as doing little snippets of writing with your child and then reading them together. If your child is in the emergent literacy stages, it is perfectly fine to write down what he or she tells you. Here are some activities and snippets to get your child writing.

Asking your child to write about his or her own life can be one way to get the writing going. Writing from life events allows you and your child to talk and write about shared experiences and time together.

- What Can You Remember? Memory Snippets
  - Write about a special day.
  - Write about a holiday.
  - Write about the first day of school.
  - Write about your birthday.
  - Write about a sports event.
  - Write about learning how to ride your bike or swim.

Writing a letter or note can be fun, especially when you add some special touches like designing the stationery or note card, stamping designs, using fun letters, and writing with special colored pens or markers (available in craft stores). Adding drawings and artwork make it even more personal. Another special addition to a note is to include your child's handprint. This simple extra item adds a special touch.

- Write a letter to a family member or friend.
  - Write a thank-you note.
  - Write to congratulate someone on an accomplishment.
  - Write to someone about a celebration.
  - Write a birthday card and note.
  - Write a holiday card and note.
  - Write a postcard or letter while traveling on vacation.
  - Add special touches like your child's handprint, "selfie" photos, or a collage made from magazine pictures that fits the theme of the note.

- For young children, it is a good idea for them to dictate their stories or writing to you. As they tell you what they want on paper, write it down. This can serve a way to model writing as well. Children can then read back what has been written.

- For older children, have them write a review of their favorite musician's latest song or a movie they have seen. Have them write a letter to the editor about a recent topic in the newspaper or a community issue that interests them. This is especially good for helping kids build argument and persuasion skills.

- Send your child a lunch box note and ask for a reply.

Books About Letter Writing:

Click, Clack, Moo: Cows That Type by Doreen Cronin (Simon & Schuster, 2000)

Dear Mr. Henshaw by Beverly Cleary (William Morrow and Company, 1983)

Dear Mrs. LaRue: Letters from Obedience School by Mark Teague (Scholastic, 2002)

The Flat Stanley Collection by Jeff Brown (HarperCollins, 2012)

The Jolly Postman by Janet & Allan Ahlberg (Heinemann, 1986)

Family Book Clubs

Book clubs are a great way for families to enjoy reading and discussing books together. Book clubs involve people meeting to discuss a book they have read and expressing their opinions, likes, dislikes, and other types of responses. It can function much like a conversation about a movie recently viewed. Book club integrates reading, listening, speaking, and thinking in authentic ways that make sense to children and parents. Research done on book clubs suggests that they not only increased reading for pleasure but improved children's higher-order thinking skills, such as analyzing and evaluating stories and the ideas in them, comprehension, and the ability to have deep discussions about topics. To get started with family book clubs:

- Pick a day and time that works for the family. If you have young children, picture books could work weekly. Chapter books for older children might require more time between club meetings.

- Let your child pick out the book club selection. You might consider providing a list of book club possibilities to choose from.

- Let your child pick snacks and drinks. Consider meeting at a restaurant or a favorite family spot.

- Invite friends and neighbors to join your book club.

- Set some ground rules, and highlight respect for each other's responses.

- Book club selection can also include informational text, nonfiction, newspaper articles, and magazines.

- Have your child keep a book club journal and write down things he or she wants to remember to bring up during book club.

- For older children and teens, encourage them to start their own book club with their friends.

Once you get your book club off and running, you might consider planning a family dinner around the theme of a book. You can have your child help you create a menu, decorations, and activities that are based on the book.

Family Dinner Book Club

The Growing Book by Book website has a terrific source for sharing great stories through family dinner book clubs. It includes menus, table crafts, conversation starters, talking points, and recommended titles.

It's OK to Turn Off the TV

In many of the interviews I have had with parents, they tell me that their children watch way too much TV and spend too much time with digital devices. One father told me that his children want the TV on all the time as background noise even when they are engaged with digital devices. He feels that his kids multitask and have no fewer than two to three activities that they are doing all at once. Another mother told me that she tries to sit and watch TV with her children and make it an active rather than passive experience. She will ask questions about what they are viewing and get her children to engage in conversations. As much as possible, she tries to monitor the viewing and encourage educational TV.

There is no question that TV can be an excellent learning tool for children to expand their knowledge base. When I work with children of all ages and they offer me in-depth information about a subject area, I ask how they know all this information. Very often they will tell me it is from watching TV, and many specifically mention the History Channel. One student in our Summer Reading Clinic was an "expert" on warships and planes. He had put together model planes and warships and shared them with his peers in class. During this sharing period, his peers would ask detailed questions about certain aspects and parts of the vehicles. He would respond with such a sophisticated knowledge base, representing facts and answering like an expert. When I asked him how he had acquired such knowledge, he said he watched the History Channel with his father. They would then try to find model kits to assemble and use the computer to find out more information about the planes and ships. He would spend hours searching for specific types of war vehicles. His parents did not view this as living literacy, however, and thought that he should be reading books instead.

When we worked with the parents and explained how all of his efforts (TV, building models, and searching for information) were contributing to his overall knowledge base, it made more sense to them. Gaining information in these ways will no doubt aid in his comprehension of text about the subject matter. This is an important example of how taking an interest and developing it into a hobby can have positive benefits on literacy and learning overall. Here are some suggestions for setting TV viewing guidelines at home:

- Base the amount of TV viewing on the ages and needs of your family members, and realize that this will need to be reevaluated often.
- Use the TV guide with your child and plan ahead to view movies, documentaries, and other educational programming.

- Watch The Weather Channel to learn about your local weather, and pay attention to key terms and concepts that the meteorologist uses.

- Remember, it is OK to turn off the TV and have quality family time for conversations and other activities.

- Watch TV with your child, and use it as an important source of gaining and learning information about the world.

- Watch movies based on books. Read the books and compare.

- Use TV to align with your child's interests, such as sports and other recreational activities.

- Watch the news together and discuss appropriate current events in your community, nation, and the world at large.

Check Out These Educational TV Channels

- **Animal Planet**
- **Discovery Channel**
- **History Channel**
- **NASA TV:** Live coverage of space walks and launches and the latest science news
- **Public Broadcasting Service (PBS):** Independently operated and nonprofit; home of *Sesame Street* and other children's programs
- **The Weather Channel**

Let's Play Games

When I was growing up, we would drive to the Michigan dunes as a family the first warm weekend in the spring. My dad would fill the trunk of his car with sand for our backyard sandbox, which led to hours and hours of play. Playing in the sandbox is all about constructing and making things. Additionally, I have fond memories of hopscotch, bike riding, hula hooping, roller skating, blowing bubbles, jumping rope, and much more. For my own children, all the above were instrumental in their development. Making tents in the backyard and inside the house on rainy days are other cozy memories I have from both my childhood and my children's. My sons loved filling their sacred spaces with favorite toys and books.

Especially for young children, playing games is a creative way to build literacy skills. Playing games makes learning fun and can include the entire family. Games help children learn how to follow directions and take turns and can strengthen reading and critical-thinking skills. Additionally, there are many ways to enhance play through talk and books. Below are some great ways to make literacy part of play and games.

Play with Literacy

Topic	Talk	Books
Hopscotch	• History of the game • Who invented it?	*Hopscotch Around the World* by Mary D. Lankford (HarperCollins, 1996)
Bubbles	• Why do bubbles pop?	*Bubbles Float, Bubbles Pop* by Mark Weakland (Capstone, 2011) *Pop! A Book about Bubbles* by Kimberly Brubaker Bradley (Baker & Taylor, CATS, 2009)
Kites	• What makes a kite fly? • Who invented the kite?	*Kite Flying* by Grace Lin (Baker & Taylor, CATS, 2009)
Hula-Hoops	• Who invented the hula hoop? • How long has it been around?	*Peggy Noodle, Hula Hoop Queen* by Dolly Dozier (Peak City Publishing, 2012)
Tents and Forts	• Who invented the tent? • Who uses a tent the most?	*A Kids' Guide to Building Forts* by Tom Birdseye (Roberts Rinehart Publishers, 1993)
Sandboxes	• Who invented the sandbox? • How long has it been around? • What types of sand are there?	*Sandbox* by Rosemary Wells (Penguin, 2010)
Jump Ropes	• Who invented the jump rope? • Why do people jump rope?	*The Kids' Guide to Jumping Rope* by Sheri Bell-Rehwoldt (Capstone, 2011)

Children love to play games, and when you can align them to a literacy activity, all the better. An activity called Finding the Evidence Game (see Appendix page 113) is designed to be used with both fiction and nonfiction selections. There is a game board with fiction and nonfiction question cards. The game pushes the child (and adult) to spend time going back into the text and finding evidence for the answer. Finding evidence from text is a major requirement of the Common Core State Standards and other state requirements, so having your child practice this in a game gets him or her ready to do it in the classroom with ease.

There are many educational games that focus on language and literacy, along with critical-thinking skills, such as Boggle and Scrabble, which both promote spelling, vocabulary, and sight words. Here are some ways you can use games to focus on literacy:

- Make a game out of your child's weekly spelling or vocabulary words (match synonyms and antonyms, words with definitions, etc.).
- For younger children, look for "junior" versions of games like Scrabble and Boggle.
- Play travel versions of games while on vacation.
- Check out garage sales and resale shops for games.
- Set aside a time for family game night.
- Watch a video on how to play hopscotch.
- Watch a video on jump rope rhymes.

Online Game Resources for Families

- **MindFun:**
  Trivia games, word puzzles, brain games, and more
- **Printable Board Games:**
  Free printable game boards and word cards that can be used for any grade level and skill
- **Discovery Education's Puzzlemaker:**
  Create your own free puzzles online

Document Literacy

We can document stories that we write, draw, or dictate in logs, journals, diaries, and memoirs. I have very sweet memories of keeping a diary while growing up and writing about special moments of my life. I remember writing "Dear diary" as if I had a special audience I was writing to, a secret unknown keeper of my life events. I have always tried to model writing at home and encouraged my children to do the same. When one of my sons was in fourth grade, I found the following notebook in his backpack. He documented his day at school and wrote about ordinary events transpiring around him.

Keeping a daily journal at home is a great way to promote authentic writing. For younger children, encourage them to draw pictures and add more text to their pictures as they progress. For older students, encourage a more detailed journal with more frequent entries or a blog written on the computer. Making a journal with a notebook and supplies for decorating it (glue, stickers, scissors, and pictures) can be fun for your child. Here are a few journals you can encourage at home:

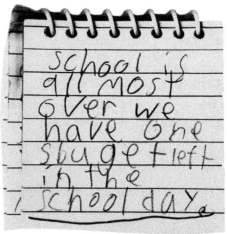

- **Appreciation Journal:** Teach your child the importance of appreciation, and model your own appreciation for everyday life. Ask your child to write about one thing he or she appreciates each day.

- **Art Journal:** Drawings and paintings can be a great way to communicate ideas and feelings. Use colored pencils, special paper, finger paints, and different types of brushes for a variety of techniques in this image-based journal.

- **Online Journal or Blog:** Blogs can provide an interactive outlet where older children and teens can post journal entries, links, pictures, and more. A blog can invite others to participate in the conversation as well.

- **Collage Journal:** Tear or cut out pictures from magazines or other sources to create a collage representing an experience, a future dream, or something more abstract. Make a collage entry from a vacation, a trip, or an experience that includes artifacts from the event (tickets, photos, maps, etc.).

- **Photo Journal:** Using photographs with text is a great way to document an experience. Children can also paste and write about photos from magazines. This can be a precious keepsake for your child.

- **Sports Journal:** Children can write about a sport they are learning or a sporting event they attended. Mementos like ticket stubs and scorecards can be pasted in the journal.

- **Travel Journal:** Chronicle the events of trip, and include photos and artifacts.

Books Written in Diary Format

- *Artichoke Hearts* by Sita Brahmachari (Macmillan, 2011)
- *Diary of a Wimpy Kid* by Jeff Kinney (Amulet Books, 2007)
- *Diary of a Wombat* by Jackie French (Houghton Mifflin Harcourt, 2002)
- *Middle School Is Worse Than Meatloaf* by Jennifer L. Holm (Simon & Schuster, 2011)
- *The Secret Diary of Adrian Mole, Aged 13¾* by Sue Townsend (Puffin, 2009)
- *Zlata's Diary* by Zlata Filipovic (Penguin, 2006)

Handmade Books

- The Making Books website offers free projects and family resources for creating handmade books (often out of recycled materials) that can be used for journals.

- Scrapbooks of photos and artifacts can document your child's interests or life events and are easy to expand as time goes on. Consider working together with your child on a scrapbook for family trips, hobbies, and other interests.

Keeping track of literacy activities that you have completed is a wonderful way to document the experience with your child, sustaining the experience over time. Post the documentation in a place like the kitchen bulletin board or refrigerator, where it can be seen and evoke conversation. Even including a list of books (title and author) that your child or the family wants to read is important. Keep different lists, such as books read aloud, books shared with each other, family book club books, and books you want to read.

Interests Matter

All of my four sons had interests that were shared (sports and building), yet all four had unique and specific interests of their own. One son was interested in digger trucks so much that a walk or drive in the neighborhood was stalled to watch a construction truck. He even managed to get a ride on one. Although this interest was short lived, we dove into many informational texts on the topic.

Another son took up dinosaurs for several years and knew every classification, name, and more. We heard about dinosaurs in our house for a long time. This same son also had an incredible interest in turtles, which caused us to purchase one as a pet. (It still lives in our kitchen.) We call him "Old Turtle" after the name of a book. Although all my sons enjoyed building with blocks, one son would go further, building complete towns with roads that would take him days to complete. None of the interests that my children had early on have led to a lifelong professional career (yet). However, I believe that their thirst for knowledge on these topics was critical and instrumental in the formation of their literacy life.

Interest is a HOOK, and when a child has an interest in any topic, one of the easiest ways to hold on to their interest is to follow up with information. (See the Interest Tracker on page 112 in the Appendix.) Information can be in the form of text, digital, or nonprint information. Sharing your child's interests with his or her teacher is important as we want classroom libraries to be full of information that aligns with all students' interests.

Each year in our Summer Reading Clinic, we ask parents to list their child's interests and hobbies. There is no question that year after year, sports top the list. We need to capitalize on that in terms of literacy and learning. Sports become the hook. There are so many ways to use sports to encourage literacy development. Older children and teens are especially interested in sports and can read biographies of coaches and sports heroes or informational text about a particular sport. Let your children's interests drive their reading choices, and help them acquire as much information as they can on their favorite topics.

Chapter Three: Home-to-school Connections

Going back to school after having the summer off or getting a preschooler ready for the first day can be a daunting experience. Living literacy at home can make the transition to school easier. Living the literacy life means that, as parents, we make a special effort to pay attention to daily activities and connect them to literacy. This chapter provides information on getting your child ready for school, not just in the fall but each day throughout the year. Ideas are provided for maintaining ongoing communication with teachers and being a school volunteer. Tips for making homework and parent-teacher conferences run as smoothly as possible are also included. The chapter ends with a special section on what do if you think your child is struggling in school.

Getting Ready for School and Other Back-to-school Ideas

Some of my favorite memories growing up were of getting ready for school. The anticipation was in the air by mid-August as we gathered school supplies and a new lunch box to start off fresh. With my own children, we spent late summer afternoons going school supply shopping. We would collect the local flyers from the retail stores, and then the children would do comparison shopping to see who had the best deals. Letting the children pick out their own notebooks, pens, and paper was an important ritual for getting ready for school. We posted the school supply list in the kitchen and checked each item off the list as it was purchased. We made something as simple as this into a family literacy activity. Family book clubs helped us complete summer reading together as did getting the books on tapes. Conversations about going back to school were also helpful.

Back-to-school Parent Talk

- "I remember thinking about the first day of school and what it would be like."
- "I'm looking forward to you starting school. I know it must be an exciting time."
- "What questions do you have about school starting?"
- "What are you most looking forward to with starting school?"

Back-to-school Planner

Planning ahead and getting organized for the start of school will help you and your family start off on the right foot. Think about all the tasks that need to get done, and break them down into more manageable jobs to be completed the month before, the week before, the day before, and the starting day. See Appendix pages 118–119 for a Back-to-school Planner. You can also start to work on the tasks listed here before the first day of school:

- Walk or drive to the school building if this is the first time attending. Let your child see the building, playground, and surroundings. Talk about the building and playground. Get familiar with your walking or driving route.

- Make sure you get your child's school supplies in advance. Make it a fun shopping experience for the family.

- Have your child label all the supplies with his or her name.

- Talk about your own experiences of going to school, and share what you remember about the first day.

- If your child seems hesitant or anxious, try to talk through the event in a calming, reassuring way, explaining that being nervous is very common.

- If your child has been sleeping later over the summer, have him or her get up and go to bed earlier at least the week before schools starts.

- Read books about the first day of school.

Books about the First Day of School

- *Little Lizard's First Day*
  by Melinda Melton Crow (Stone Arch Books, 2011)
- *My First Day at a New School*
  by Charlotte Guillain (Heinemann-Raintree, 2011)
- *My First Day at School*
  by Rebecca Hunter (Evans Brothers, 2010)

Communication Is Key: Strategies for Ongoing Communication with Teachers

In our Summer Reading Clinic, we make every effort to ensure communication with parents is a priority. Drop-off and pick-up is a time where brief conversations happen and feedback is provided. No doubt, communication is vital to home and school partnerships. You will need to decide how much communication is necessary for you and your child, and you will want to respect the school's policy regarding e-mail and teacher contact. If you receive newsletters and frequent communication from the teacher and school, you may decide that scheduled parent-teacher conferences and open houses are all that you need. On the other hand, you might feel you need to know more and request additional communication. Do what feels comfortable to you. Both parents and teachers know and sense when communication is lacking in a home-school partnership. According to Lilly and Green (2004), your child's teacher will benefit from home-school partnerships by understanding your child and family and "gaining insights into the family situations that might influence children's behavior and learning at school." To foster good parent-teacher communication:

- Let your child's teacher know that you are available for communicating via e-mail, phone calls, and face-to-face meetings. Provide the best time to reach you and your contact information.

- When you have a question or need an issue resolved, make an appointment to discuss it with the teacher. Drop-off and pick-up might not be an appropriate or sufficient venue for longer conversations.

- Always respect the teacher's time, and remember that your child's teacher might have 30 families or more in one classroom with whom to communicate.

Be a Volunteer and Get Involved in Your Child's School

My mother was a frequent school volunteer and active member of the Parent Teacher Association (PTA). I remember her volunteering in the cafeteria on special days, and her participation in my school was important to me. I was an active volunteer in my children's schools. In fact, the best part of school volunteering was forging lifelong friendships with other parents. As a room parent, I was able to meet new people and develop friendships. I still get together with those "room moms." These relationships are priceless to me and would not have happened without my volunteer role. The other benefits of volunteering in your child's school are plenty. There is an opportunity to interact with the teachers, staff, and school leaders. You get to see firsthand the school day in action. Moreover, you can have casual conversations in real time with teachers, which can be critical communication. Adams (2015) reports that "parent involvement, regardless of income, race, or ethnicity, contributes to better grades, attendance, and graduate rates." More recently, Goldstein (2015) talks about the merits of volunteering in schools, making it a more positive place for kids, but also a way to be a good citizen. Here are some tips on volunteering in your child's school:

- Talk to your child about being a volunteer. Ask how he or she feels about your participation in the school and how comfortable he or she will be with you there.

- Let your child's teacher know that you are willing to volunteer for field trips and other school events.

- Share with your child's teacher any special talents that you have and feel you would like to share with the class (artist, photographer, musician, party planner, graphic designer, writer, etc.). Some teachers encourage this kind of classroom participation, and it may also be easier for you to offer help outside of school events.

- Check with the school library and see if volunteers are needed to read aloud to the children or assist in other tasks (career talks, teach-ins, book drives, etc.).

- Get involved in the parent organizations (PTA, PTO, school councils, and others) by attending meetings, being on committees, or running for an organizational office.

- Some schools have lunchroom and playground volunteers, so check to see if this is a possibility in your child's school.

- Some schools have room parents assigned to each classroom to assist in helping out with class parties and events.

- Talk to the school leaders about setting up a **parent library** at the entrance of the school. This is a terrific way to provide access to books for families.

- If your school has a family literacy night, volunteer for it. If the school does not have such an event, discuss the possibility with school leaders.

The parent library is a foundational library that can set the tone for the new balanced literacy school. When the school entranceway is transformed into a space that creates access to books for parents and the community at large, it sends an important message about family literacy and home-school partnerships. Creating a literate environment that includes the parents and community is critical for school-wide literacy success. The bridge between home and school is one that should be promoted and celebrated each day in your child's school (Policastro & McTague, 2015).

Surviving Homework and Other Strategies

"Homework has been part of students' lives since the beginning of formal schooling in the United States. However, the practice has sometimes been accepted and other times rejected, both by educators and parents. This has happened because homework can have both positive and negative effects on children's learning and attitudes toward school" (U.S. Department of Education, 2003).

When I think back on doing homework while growing up, it was something that, for the most part, I looked forward to and enjoyed. Tasks like book reports, workbook pages, and hands-on projects could be done independently after school. By fourth or fifth grade, I would stop at the public library on the way home from school and get as much done as possible. One vivid homework memory involved gathering leaves as a family for a science leaf collection. We drove around parks picking up as many new and different leaves as possible. My parents were always on call to assist and support with homework, especially difficult or challenging tasks that needed explanation and scaffolding. When homework started with my own children, very often it seemed like a juggling act between preparing dinner, attending sports practices, going to other after-school events, and squeezing in my own work. Finding quality time for homework was something we had to work on as a family, but it was worth the effort and made that time more enjoyable.

In an interview with a father of three children who was born in Ecuador and now lives in Chicago, Illinois, I was struck by our conversation as he shared with me the painful experiences of growing up and going to school in Ecuador. He recounted endless times of being punished for things like erasing too much on his paper with his pencil. These experiences have caused him to have a negative outlook on schooling for his own children in America, and he feels very disconnected from his children's educational experiences. In fact, he often feels helpless when it comes to helping with homework and other school activities. He feels he can't help out with homework because he was taught in such a different way.

Another parent I interviewed is a mother from Mexico. She told me how difficult homework has been for her and her three children. She said, "Even kindergarten homework was too difficult for me because of the language differences." This mother feels that her own children can't count on her for help. Although she is an avid volunteer in the school, she can't assist her own children with academic work. She went on to say that she encourages her children to pay attention and ask the teacher when they don't understand information or assignments.

Our own school experiences have shaped our beliefs and perceptions about school for our children. Recently, a school principal shared with me that many parents in her school did not have good educational experiences and come to their children's school with negative outlooks. This principal went on to say that working with parents is a high priority. Principals, teachers, and other school support staff are there to help, but parents need to try to have a positive attitude toward their children's school and make an effort to put aside their own negative school experiences. Consider setting up a meeting with the principal or teacher to discuss your own experiences and concerns to put you at ease and figure out next steps.

Having more than one child can also affect the dynamics of getting homework completed. One mother told me that she had to create a special space for her daughter, so she is not disturbed by her younger brother. Taking the dynamics of all the members of your family into consideration will help you plan for homework each year. Keep in mind that the situation will change as your child gets older.

My sons are eight years apart from oldest to youngest, so you can imagine what this spread looked like for homework completion tasks. If you have older children, much needs to be taken into consideration. The homework center needs to accommodate more than one child. Older children can be a great asset in helping their younger siblings complete homework tasks, including reading to the younger child or listening to the younger one read. Older children might want to work in bedrooms or other quiet spaces away from others. Juggling the tasks of each child's homework and needs requires special attention to detail and lots of planning. The more organized and proactive you are, the smoother the process will go each day.

Homework can help foster greater understanding and communication between teachers and families. Parents gain insight into what is being taught in the classroom, and teachers learn about the family dynamics of their students. Parents should view homework as a positive experience and model a confident attitude toward the value of completing work and succeeding in school. Consider these homework guidelines:

Set up a Homework Center

- Create a homework center where your child can study quietly at the same time each day without distractions.

- Be close enough to the homework space in order to monitor and be available for help and support.

- Have access to computers and printers at the homework center.

- Set up a homework center supply box that includes all the necessary things to complete homework assignments and projects; replenish often.

- Use bright lighting and ensure a low noise level in the homework center.

- Organize homework assignments at the beginning of a homework session.

- Use an age-appropriate assignment notebook and plan adequately for short- and long-term assignments.

- Hang a homework calendar in the kitchen, and post assignment due dates as soon as they are assigned.

- Have wall hooks near the homework center. This will keep the workspace less cluttered and also allow for a place to store backpacks.

Helpful Hints

- Take homework seriously, and be sure to make it a family priority.

- Get an assignment notebook for your child, and teach him or her how to use it.

- Set aside time each day for homework and assume that there will be assignments to complete. Plan a homework schedule/routine.

- Talk about homework assignments with your child, and let him or her know that you have high expectations. Encourage your child to ask questions and be an advocate for him or herself, especially when unsure of how to complete a homework assignment.

- Use homework as a way to teach your child about time management. With your child, estimate how long assignments will take to complete and plan accordingly. Often, children will underestimate the time needed to complete a homework assignment.

- Provide feedback and watch for any signs of your child getting frustrated during the homework assignment.

- Provide guidance without taking over your child's homework.

- Turn off the TV during homework time.

- Be sure to provide breaks and free time during homework.

- Don't give answers; rather, provide clues and information to help your child seek out the answer or solve the problem.

- Don't hesitate to contact your child's teacher if your child experiences difficulty in understanding an assignment. This happens to many children, and teachers are happy to help.

- After-school playdates can include getting the homework completed.

- Try to get homework done at a reasonable time, so your child can still relax and have some downtime.

- Develop a plan for getting homework if your child is absent from school. A homework buddy can be a big help so your child does not fall behind.

- Consider ordering a set of textbooks to keep at home. Often these books can be purchased used and at a reduced price. This will help if your child forgets a book needed for the assignment.

Parent-Teacher Conferences and How to Be Prepared

Another important dimension to teacher communication and the home-school partnership is the parent-teacher conferences scheduled during the year. Getting ready for these conferences can be stressful, especially if you are not sure what to expect. There are several important things to consider when getting ready for attending a conference. You should begin to plan for the conference ahead of time so that going will not feel overwhelming. If this is your first conference with the teacher, be prepared to listen to the teacher and learn about how your child is progressing in the classroom. It will be helpful for you to go with a plan that includes questions you have and any questions that your child might have as well. Conferences are generally 10–15 minutes in length, so coming prepared will help you make the best use of your time and the teacher's time.

Every summer in our clinic, we ask parents to tell us how their child learns best. We ask this question because we feel that parents do indeed know how their child learns and what preferences they have for learning. Some responses from parents are on the next page.

How Does Your Child Learn Best?	
Visual learner	Interactive learning
Hands-on	Pictures and explanations
Motivated to learn	Small group setting
Encouraged and challenged	Visual and auditory learner
Having fun and being creative	Through games
Support and encouragement	Alone or in a small group
One-on-one	By doing
Slow pace and interaction with the teacher	Small settings with few distractions

Take some time to think about how your child learns best. You should consider sharing this information with your child's teacher. Planning for the parent-teacher conference should include your goals and priorities, detailing what you expect to get from the conference.

Before the Conference

Write down questions and concerns you would like to discuss with the teacher. Rank them by which are most important to be answered. Ask your child if he or she has questions about school you can gladly ask about during the conference. Think about what information you would like to share with the teacher. This might include circumstances that are important for the teacher to know (your child's learning preferences, attitudes, interests, hobbies, and any other special family information). As you prepare for the conference, get a notebook or folder so you can have the information readily available at the conference. This also provides a place for you to take notes. If you have more than one child's conference to attend, this requires extra organization and planning, especially if the conferences are scheduled back-to-back. Try to understand the schedule, know how much time there is between appointments, and learn where the classrooms are beforehand. Be sure to let the teachers know you have more than one conference to attend. Remember to schedule a babysitter if needed, and have him or her arrive at your house early so that you are not rushed.

During the Conference

Listen carefully to what the teacher tells you about your child. Take notes so you don't have to worry about remembering everything. Be ready to ask questions about anything you might be uncertain of or want to know more about. Ask the questions that you brought with you if they haven't already been answered. Share with the teacher information that you feel is important for the school to know. Things like your child's hobbies and reading interests are always a good to share, as well as how you think your child learns best. Be sure to ask about volunteer opportunities, and let the teacher know you are available to help out. Ask about any special things you can do at home to assist your child in learning.

Parent Talk for Conferences

- "I was wondering about volunteer activities that I might be able to get involved with in the school. Can you help me with this?"
- "My child has a few questions about _____ (homework, tests, etc.)."
- "I was wondering how we can communicate about homework if there is a problem. Do you have an e-mail address, and is it okay to e-mail you?"

After the Conference

Share what you have learned from the teacher with your child. Talk about expectations that the teacher might have shared with you. Give yourself time to reflect on the information you learned at the conference. If you have follow-up questions, be sure to send them to the teacher. Consider ways to maintain ongoing communication with the teacher.

When Your Child Is Struggling in School

I am frequently contacted by parents who are concerned about some aspect of their child's literacy development. The following are some common issues parents have shared with me over the years:

- My child doesn't like to read.

- My child won't read anything on his own.

- My child starts a book or an article but doesn't finish it.

- My child has a hard time doing homework assignments.

- My child seems behind in reading.

- My child does not enjoy writing and has difficulty writing anything.

- We have to sit one-on-one with our child in order to get him or her to do homework.

- My child's test scores are below grade level.

- I think my child has a learning disability.

- My child can't pay attention during reading.

Parents feel very frustrated, stressed, and uncertain about what to do. One thing you can do is keep track of the behaviors or things that you notice, including dates. This is a way you can show progress or a pattern of falling behind. Be in contact with your child's teacher and share your concerns. You might schedule follow-up meetings with the teacher to see how your child is doing. Most important, you want to continue to provide support and encouragement to your child.

This struggling can be short- or long-term. An example of a temporary struggle could be a student who is unmotivated and has no interest in reading. Children need to feel successful in their literacy development, and reading and writing must be a process they enjoy. When a child is not successful in school, too often he or she develops a lack of motivation or interest in reading and writing. Seeking out the child's interests and hobbies and presenting him or her with more books of interest can encourage motivation, confidence, and success.

A long-term struggle might have to do with issues of attention or a diagnosed learning disability. In either case, the struggle needs to be addressed by both the parent and the school. Perhaps some testing needs to be done or the child needs to meet with a specialist.

Another scenario is when your child's teacher or school notifies you that your child is struggling with some aspect of literacy development. Such notification might include the following:

- Your child is not paying attention in class.

- Your child can't keep up with the rest of the class.

- Your child does not seem interested in school or learning.

- Your child is reluctant to show work.

- Your child does not complete class work on time.

- Your child does not complete homework on time.

- Your older child is reading at a lower grade level.

I recently worked with a boy who was diagnosed with severe learning disabilities. His handwriting was illegible, so written language was a problem. He could not calculate, so math was another problem. However, he played computer and video games with no difficulty and was most interested in anything that had to do with gaming. To address his expressive language issues, he would dictate to me his thoughts, and I would do the writing. I realized his mind was so full of information, and he just needed a way to be able to express it. Over time and with practice, his ability to express his own thoughts using a computer increased. Once he was able to generate text on his own, we worked on spelling, grammar, and other issues that he lagged far behind on. Confidence can certainly play a critical role when a student is not having success in school early on. Day after day of unsuccessful attempts can cause a child to shut down and not want to participate in the learning process within the classroom. What might be perceived as a lack of interest or motivation can actually be a sign of a more difficult problem. Getting to the root of the problem and finding ways to assist the student in how he or she learns best is critical to future development and success. It took several years of working with this student in one-on-one sessions to achieve success. He gradually was able to do his work independently, and we went over it to make sure it was as close to correct as possible.

I interviewed a mother who had concerns about her daughter, a kindergartner, and was referred to a specialist for an assessment. The family was worried that she might be on the autism spectrum or have learning disabilities. The referral process and going to the actual assessment was frightening for the family. But communication was kept open, there were interventions put in place, and now the child is thriving. Parents often feel helpless and do not know where to turn or what to do. Parents feel especially frustrated when they seem to have no options or network for support. As a parent, be proactive and seek a referral to see if outside assistance is needed. Start with the school for these referrals to see if there are other learning issues interfering with your child's progress. You are your child's first and best advocate, but the school has a support team to help you.

Maturity is another factor that affects learning development. Some children are the youngest in the class and have not had the same amount of time to mature. In some classrooms, there can be a three-year age range between students.

Emotional, social, and physical or health factors play a role in learning as well. When I was teaching reading in the public schools, I had a fourth-grade student who was struggling from missing most of the beginning reading instruction because he needed glasses. It wasn't until the end of second grade that his visual impairment was identified. The problem was addressed and he got glasses, but he needed to catch up. A mother shared a similar story in which her child was behind in reading due to a hearing impairment. Once the issue was discovered and addressed, he was on his way to learning.

One other factor to consider is how your child learns best and how this learning style is aligned to the teaching style within the classroom. Some children need more time, more explanation, hands-on practice, or other accommodations to fit their style of learning. Here's what you can do to address learning issues early on and effectively:

- Talk to your child's teacher about your concerns, and determine if extra help is needed.

- Set up follow-up meetings to track progress and get frequent feedback.

- Talk to the school counselor or social worker for more information, and discuss whether you might need outside referrals.

- Get referrals from other parents who have been given similar assessments.

- Talk with your child's pediatrician about your concerns and referrals.

- If you are not able to get your child assessed through the school, you might consider private assessments.

- Be patient, and know that sometimes there is no quick fix. The solution can take time to unfold as different areas are addressed.

Chapter Four: Access to Books

Growing up, we had one bookcase in our house and it was full of Hardy Boys books, Nancy Drew books, Bobbsey Twins Books, and some scouting books and handbooks. The bookcase also held a special collection of six books titled *The Child's World*, a set that my mother bought from a door-to-door salesman. This set had six hardback books with amazing glossy pages of gorgeous photographs. Between weekly trips to the public library and our tiny home library, I was set on a literacy adventure that continues today.

Harste, Woodward & Burke (1984) make the point that young children will certainly benefit when they are surrounded by and exposed to an environment rich in print. A print-rich environment includes books, newspapers, magazines, and all other print-related sources in the home. I believe that year-round access to books is critical to literacy success for all children. Access to books in a print-rich home is a major contributor to children's interests, attitudes, and motivation toward reading. Access to books for parents, grandparents, caregivers, and children is a central theme of this book.

This model begins with the home library, which is centrally located so family members all have easy access to the collection. From the larger home library, other smaller libraries can meet specific needs. For young children, a bedtime story library is the perfect way to get your child off to sleep. Access to books near your child's bed will make it easy to share books together and read stories aloud. Books and print materials in other rooms of your home will be a constant reminder of the opportunities to interact with print.

Building a Home Library

Several years ago, I made the decision to centrally locate my children's entire book collection (several thousand). This collection is larger than what is typical because I teach a children's literature class and need to be current in the field. After much deliberation, a library was created to hold my collection (pictured here). Creating a special place for books shows your children the importance of reading. Creating a home library can be a fun, simple project that will produce endless learning opportunities for your family. The home library that we created was made out of a small room with French doors to allow light. The floor-to-ceiling shelving was constructed from cabinets without doors. There are two small, half-circle, curved desks on each side, which allow for quiet study and book browsing. Wood flooring and a carpet turned the library into a literacy sanctuary. The shelves are filled with special books, autographed copies, and writing journals. Additional small baskets are filled with books, family pictures, and artifacts to add a special touch.

Access and Location

Think about where your library will be created. The location for your home library is everything. Bring all family members into the discussion and planning, so everyone has a voice in the decision. Think about the location as a quiet and cozy place where your child will be able to curl up with a book or do homework. Some good spaces to consider include corners in your family room, living room, basement, or office. Think about the size of the library and how much space you actually need. Consider how to bring in natural light and what the seating arrangement will entail.

After giving a workshop on building home libraries to parents at our Summer Reading clinic, one mother transformed her living room space into a home library. She took two medium-sized bookshelves and centrally located books, games, and other educational materials on the shelves as well. She also included a small square table with four chairs, where homework could be completed. She added organizational containers for materials and decorated the walls with framed artwork from her children. The corner was full of beanbag chairs and other children's furniture to make it as inviting as possible.

Supplies

The supplies for your home library depend on the mood you would like to create and how you plan to organize your books. A few suggestions include comfy beanbag chairs, an armchair, and a rocking chair. Think about a carpet or an area rug to keep the walking noise quiet. Bookshelves, bins, and baskets all work well for storage and can help you organize books by series or specialty.

Collection

When selecting books for your home library, it will be important to choose a wide variety of books that meet your family's interests and ages. Be sure to include different genres and nonfiction as well as fiction. Informational texts that meet interests are always a good start. Book series and favorite authors and illustrators should all be taken into consideration. For older children, chapter books should be well stocked and added to the collection often. When selecting books for your home library, remember that not all of the books need to be brand new. Places to purchase used books include garage and yard sales, public library book sales, used bookstores, resale shops, and online sites.

Possible Collection Ideas

- picture books
- realistic fiction: books on diversity and world cultures, animal stories, sports stories, mysteries
- folktales, fables, myths
- fantasy and modern fairy tales
- historical fiction
- science fiction
- nonfiction books: concept books, picture books, specialized books, craft books
- poetry
- biographies
- magazines and newspapers

Technology and the Home Library

Technology supports literacy and should be an important component in the development of the home library. This space should be a place where children can access electronic text. This will be especially important for older children and teens as they read on e-readers and computers and use cell phones to access the world. Technology has become an important part of learning and should be promoted in the home.

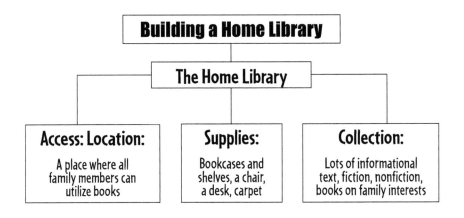

Building a Home Library

The Home Library

Access: Location:
A place where all family members can utilize books

Supplies:
Bookcases and shelves, a chair, a desk, carpet

Collection:
Lots of informational text, fiction, nonfiction, books on family interests

The Home Library: A Checklist

Access: location	☐ A place that all family members can utilize ☐ A place that is quiet and free from distractions
Supplies	☐ Shelving/bookcases/bins/baskets for books ☐ Bookends ☐ A desk and chair for technology and writing ☐ A cozy chair or sofa for reading ☐ A carpet
Collection	☐ Lots of informational texts ☐ Fiction and nonfiction ☐ Classics ☐ Books that meet family interests ☐ Storybooks and other reading for bedtime

The Bedtime Story Library and Collection

One way to encourage nightly reading is to provide access to books near your child's bed. A bedtime story library doesn't need to be elaborate. Rather, it should have enough space to make nighttime books available.

- Tuck some books under the pillow in the morning, and surprise your child with a different selection each night.
- Keep a basket of books near the bed for easy access.
- Set up a small bookcase that is dedicated to bedtime reading.
- Include big and little books, fiction, and nonfiction.

Places for Books in the Home

A mother told me recently that she was concerned that her child, a voracious reader, would read in the bathroom. When I told her that a basket of books in the bathroom is a great way to engage kids in reading (especially at bath time), she was relieved. In addition to the bathroom, just about every room in your home can handle a space for books. With just a little planning, each room can have its own special book holdings. The kitchen is a perfect place for books about cooking, food, gardening, and nature. A small bookcase or shelf is perfect. Living rooms and family rooms can also hold books of interest.

Newspapers, Magazines, and Other Print Sources

Growing up, we had the newspaper delivered to our doorstep each day. My mother and father were eager to read every page. I have memories of the Sunday newspaper and all the additional sections (especially the comics) that I never missed. My mother also received a newspaper in Polish that she enjoyed looking at. I remember trying to read the captions below the pictures to figure out what the article was about. In our home, my children couldn't wait to read the sports section each day from start to finish.

Most recently, we did a workshop for parents and children in our Summer Reading Clinic on using the newspaper at home and were pleasantly surprised by the outcome. We put newspapers on the tables and asked the parents to interact with their children. Instantly, the room buzzed with engaging conversations. Parents were pointing out headlines, pictures, and other parts within sections. We were a bit surprised to learn that many of the families didn't get a paper newspaper delivered but rather read an electronic version. After the workshop, parents said they were definitely going to get the newspaper delivered to their homes as a way to "live literacy."

Newspapers are a great way to foster family discourse or discussions about the world. They can spark real debates about important current issues and events. Instructional shifts include students reading at least 50 percent informational and complex text. Newspapers provide the perfect way to combine your child's interests with current issues in an informational text format.

- With younger children, start with an article title (making sure that it is appropriate for your child's age) and discuss predictions of what the article might be about. Use the pictures to predict and/or infer what the information will be about.
- Point out the different sections of the newspaper, and see if your child shows an interest in a particular category of news. Many newspapers have sections written especially for kids.
- Talk about how reading the newspaper is a different kind of reading experience and has a different purpose from reading books.
- Get into the routine of reading some sections or headlines out load and other sections silently. Your child will no doubt find an area of interest to read silently.
- For older children, ask questions about information within the newspaper and request evidence in the response.
- Debate and discuss an article to show how you don't always have to agree with an author. Editorial sections of the newspaper are great for starting these kinds of discussions.
- Focus on the photographs within the newspaper, and discuss their alignment to the article.
- Use the newspaper as a way for your child to keep up with current events in the world and your local community.
- Ask questions about a particular feature and make connections to your family. Ask for reactions from your child.

Like newspapers, magazines are another great way to keep literacy alive in your home. Kids anticipate the new issue arriving each month. I have wonderful memories of walking home from school, hoping that the latest issue of my subscription had arrived. It had crafts, short stories, and paper dolls and clothes to cut out each month. While writing this book, my brother reminded me that he received *Boys' Life* each month while he was in scouting. Like newspapers, magazines have short feature articles and are lightweight and portable.

Magazines for Children and Teens

- *Highlights* (ages 2–6)
- *Ladybug* (ages 3–6)
- *Cricket* (ages 9–14)
- *Boys' Life* (ages 7–17)
- *Girls' Life* (tweens and teens)
- *Seventeen* (teens)

Don't throw out your family magazines before taking a look at the pictures. Using pictures to teach comprehension skills can be a fun activity. Allowing your child to predict what might have happened before, during, and after the action portrayed in a picture will help develop and build both prediction and sequencing skills (Policastro, 1985). These skills are important in the development of literacy within the classroom. Cut out pictures from your old magazines that have bright and colorful action and information within the photograph. The pictures can depict scenes of children, adults, nature, and more. Use these pictures to ask your child what might have taken place before the picture. Where might the people have been? What did they do to get to where they are now? Ask your child what is happening during the picture, and then try to get him or her to think ahead and take the event one step further. What do you think will happen next to the people or situation in the picture? What are the next actions they could take? Even encourage your child to guess or make up an event that could happen.

Online News Sources and News Magazines

- CNN Student News (online news and videos for students)
- Dogo News (kid-friendly site with stories, pictures, videos, world events, sports, music, entertainment, and more)
- Government for Kids (online source of government information for kids)
- Newsela (online news for kids specifically intended to build reading comprehension)
- *Sports Illustrated Kids* (sports for kids)
- *TIME for Kids* (a news magazine just for kids)

Decorating with Books

It wasn't until I was a reading teacher and had my own classroom that I saw the potential of decorating a space with books. In schools, we don't refer to it as decorating with books, but rather creating a literate environment. As a teacher, I was amazed at how a whole room, section of a room, or corner could be transformed by simply standing a hardcover book up so the cover and title are facing out for all to see. This works quite well on a windowsill, shelf, or table. When my own children were young, this idea was transferred into their bedrooms and the playroom. I made a special effort to find books that would be appealing and invite the looker to pick them up. As a parent, you want to advertise the books in your home by displaying books all over. Think about how access to books in this manner will provide reading at your child's fingertips.

Using children's books to decorate for seasons and the holidays makes the selections even more fun and timely. Display books about trees, leaves, and the fall harvest for autumn. For winter, use books about snow. For spring and summer, add books about planting seeds, flowers blooming, butterflies, clouds, rain, the beach, and picnics. One grandmother who I visited had arranged stand-up books from the entryway of her home to the living room, kitchen, and hallways. The children's books all had a holiday theme and were so inviting even adults were looking at them. Pop-up books add lots of visual appeal to a table. If you have an entryway with a bench or table, be sure to decorate it with some books. A mud room is a great place to greet your child with a new book. Here are other book-decorating ideas:

- Strategically locate stacks of books and magazines, and use them as conversation starters.

- Choose a weekly stand-up book to discuss, and ask kids to predict what it might be about before reading it.

- Use cookbook stands to display books.

- Have bins or baskets of books throughout your house for easy access in bedrooms and popular gathering spots.

- Have a basket of books in the bathroom to encourage your child to read while the bathtub fills up.

- Get a special box, bin, or basket for newspapers.

Where to Find Books and How to Select Books

Finding my own books has been a life quest that I love. Growing up, I usually found books at the public library. I remember that my sixth-grade teacher also had a classroom library from where we could check out books. Finding books for my personal reading, classroom teaching, and home is a constant joy. Browsing the stacks in the library or a bookstore for the right book is something I look forward to doing. When selecting books for your child or home library, it is important to be resourceful. Not all books need to be brand new. You might consider adding a tiny library or a Little Free Library to your neighborhood or community. These libraries are scattered about in different places, such as parks or outside religious centers, so people can easily take a book and add a book. This is a great way to recycle books and keep a new supply coming into your home. The concept of the Little Free Library began in 2009 to build literacy-friendly neighborhoods and promote a love of reading through free book exchanges. There are more than 30,000 of these free libraries around the world. Bookstores, libraries, garage and yard sales, resale stores, and online auction or resale sites are other good venues for books.

When trying to find the right book to pique your child's interest, the two sites below will help you find sports books, picture books, adventure books, animal books, chapter books, and much more.

- Carol Hurst's Children's Literature Site: Recommended books with reviews, ideas for using them, and much more.

- Trelease on Reading: Book lists and reviews of new titles, along with free brochures and information about reading aloud to your child.

Part of selecting books with and for your child includes finding a book that is just right: not too hard and not too easy. You want to make sure the book does not frustrate your child to the point of stopping the reading. Easy books are fine, but what you really want are books that keep your child's interest and continue to boost his or her learning. The Goldilocks Method (Ohlhausen & Jepsen, 1992), explained on the next page, can help your child choose a just-right book.

Too Easy Books

Have you read this book a lot of times before?

Do you understand the story really well?

Do you know almost every word?

Can you read it smoothly?

Too Hard Books

Are there a lot of words you can't figure out?

Are you confused about what is happening in the book?

When you read, does it sound pretty choppy?

Just Right Books

The book is interesting to you.

You can figure out most of the words in the book.

You heard the book read aloud.

You have read other books by the author.

You have someone to help you if you don't understand.

You know something about the subject.

There will be times when your child might want a book that seems too hard or too easy or that has already been read by him or her. It is OK for a child to pick a book that is too difficult. Good readers learn how to figure out information and words they don't know from the context. The context could include images, graphs, charts, or surrounding sentences. One mother of a fifth grader told me that her son had read a chapter book three times. She felt that he needed to expand his reading. The book he was reading was about survival in the wilderness, so we worked on finding books with the same themes. Some children will gravitate toward the same books. Try to find similar books and gradually increase the level of difficulty. It is important to remember that, even if a book is too hard, too easy, or repeated, you continue to keep your child interested in reading.

I often hear from parents that their child never finishes a book. One thing to remember is that adult readers start and don't finish books for legitimate reasons. It could be the reader just didn't like the book, lost interest in the book, or became bored with the subject. For children who don't finish books, suggest shorter selections, like articles, that will allow a feeling of accomplishment when completed while still maintaining interest. Help your child keep track of the selections read so he or she can see the progress in the amount of reading completed.

Weekends and Literacy

Weekends are a special time for families to regroup from the school and work week—a time to relax and rejuvenate. Weekends are also a natural time to participate in some literacy activities as a family. With schedules slowed down, weekends can be a good time to discuss books, see movies, and attend plays, sports events, and more. Entertainment is an important part of weekends and lends itself naturally to literacy activities. Often parents will ask me if they should read the book before seeing the movie with their children. Recently, I went to a ballet and had not read the book that the ballet was based on. I was so intrigued by the ballet and the information in the playbill that I read the book and then saw the ballet again. Not having read the book before I saw the ballet didn't hinder my interest or my understanding. In fact, it piqued my interest, which lead me to the book. When I saw the ballet for the second time, I felt that I could enjoy it for different reasons and was more engaged in the dancers as characters, knowing more background about their roles. Another example is from a student who said she saw the first Harry Potter movie and was inspired to then read the book. She thought the book was much more interesting than the movie. There really is no right or wrong order when it comes to reading books and seeing movies. Mixing it up can be fun, and comparing the book to the movie or the play is especially enjoyable. Comparing and contrasting is an important skill students need, and doing so with books, movies, and plays is natural. For older children, critiquing, analyzing, and summarizing are all good skills to weave into weekend entertainment.

Growing up, Sunday mornings were spent reading the paper. We all seemed to have our special sections. With my own sons, a part of Sunday mornings were also reserved for the newspaper. There is something about the Sunday edition that makes it special. Perhaps the added sections and length make it appealing. I have noticed that with my sons, the newspaper is still a daily activity in their lives as lifelong readers. Take advantage of the extra free time that weekends offer for family literacy time with these activities:

- Find coupons in the Sunday newspaper with your child.

- Do the crossword puzzles in the Sunday newspaper with your child.

- Visit the public library on the weekend for movies that can be checked out, story times, movie nights, concerts, and other family events.

- See what you can learn about your family heritage, and get to know your family roots by researching genealogy with your child. Conduct interviews with grandparents, cousins, and other living relatives. Put together a family tree to share with relatives.

- Write and illustrate a book together, using either an original idea or a favorite story as a model.

Teens and Libraries

Public libraries have made special efforts to draw in and keep teens reading. To this end, many libraries have created special teen spaces. Some libraries have teen advisory groups that advise the librarians on book collections and more. Teens are involved in writing and sharing book reviews to encourage peers to read. Other special offerings for teens include after-school, weekend, and summer activities. Some libraries have book-a-thons, overnight book events on the weekend, and movie and book club nights. Libraries also celebrate Teen Read Week, sponsored by the American Library Association (ALA). Libraries often offer teens volunteer and community service opportunities, ranging from helping younger students with homework and reading to younger students to assisting seniors and the visually impaired with reading and book selection. Some libraries offer buddy or partner reading time, in which older children read to younger children or they take turns reading to each other. To build early readers' confidence with reading aloud, some libraries have a program in which children read to therapy or service dogs. The kids can even earn prizes after completing a certain number of reading sessions to this furry—yet nonjudgmental—audience.

Museums are a nice weekend attraction for families as they provide "the perfect opportunity to learn together" (Greene, Magarity & Toth, 1998). In my hometown, there were not a lot of museums to experience. With my own sons, we made an effort to visit museums as often as possible on the weekends. Children's museums were especially popular as they offered opportunities to build things, create, explore, and have a rich overall experience. I continue to be a huge fan of museums, specifically the special and traveling exhibits, as they have so much to offer. Many museums offer guidebooks for children and families to use during their visit. They also offer after-school, weekend, and summer programming. Remember that museums cover artistic, cultural, historical, scientific, nature, children's, botanical, and zoological themes.

Summer Reading and Access to Books

The first day that school was out for the summer, I would ride my bike to the public library and enroll in the summer reading program. Each time I read a book and returned it, the librarian would put a sticker on my program chart. Once the individual chart was complete with books read, it was placed in the library window. I loved riding my bike past the library to see my completed chart on display. Libraries and some bookstores still offer incentive programs like these with prizes awarded upon completion.

When my children accompanied me to the Summer Reading Clinic, they were exposed to books and reading opportunities galore. There is no question that parents understand the importance of reading over the summer. I get calls and inquiries year-round about summer reading opportunities. Parents often tell me they are concerned about finding the right programs so their children are being productive in their literacy development over the summer. I met a mother and her three children who moved to the Chicago area from Alabama for the summer

so they could attend our clinic. During a recent summer, a family commuted two hours each way to attend. As Allington and McGill-Franzen (2013) explain, reading loss can occur during the summer break when children are not enrolled in school. Lindsey (2013) makes the argument that access to books is especially important during the summertime when children are unable to obtain books from their classroom. This loss of reading achievement is now referred to as the "summer slide," and it's important to combat with lots of summer literacy experiences. In fact, summer is the perfect time to enjoy backyards and other outdoor spaces, which naturally spark literacy-rich conversations, curiosity, and inquiry from children.

Backyard Sights and Activities	Topics of Conversation
Swings and slides	• Motion and how swings work • History of the swing and slide • Who invented them and when
Sandbox	• Who invented the sandbox • Things to make in the sand
Garden	• Planning where and what • Predicting what will happen • Discussing types of plants and produce
Birds	• Different kinds of birds • Distinctive features • Habitats • Survival and food
Magnifying glass	• How it works • Functions • Who uses it and why

Living near a lake and a pond, my family spent endless hours near water during the summer. My sons were fascinated with sand, water, frogs, fish, and any living creature they could find. They would huddle around bugs, were intrigued by natural mysteries, and asked questions nonstop. Often, I would just sit back and marvel in the continuous conversations and dialogue going on between them. They would be talking, pointing, and staring in awe of many things. It was their focused conversation that always caught my attention as they dissected dead creatures and seemed to know more about anatomy than I ever knew was possible. It is important for children to have these open-ended opportunities to explore and have adventures in nature as their curiosity about the world around them expands and grows. One of my sons still loves to go fishing. The minute he comes back into town, the fishing poles are out and he is in my backyard digging for worms. Recently, I went with him on a fishing expedition near our house. I was amazed at the knowledge he has acquired about fish and fishing. I had no idea that from all the years fishing in the harbor, his knowledge base had expanded so much—an eye-opening moment for me for sure. He knew the names of all the fish and so many other details I never knew he knew.

The summer is always a good time for children to collect things. My children were collectors of many items. They spent endless hours looking for baseball cards, finding just the right one, and learning how much it was worth. Sports cards have so much information on them that draw children's attention, including team facts and player statistics. Sports cards, small toy cars, rocks, shells, bugs, and more are delightful collections that entertain while increasing knowledge of the world. Our summer travels as a family seemed to always take us near water, and that continues to this day. Early on, my sons were intrigued with lighthouses along the shores. We would take pictures and buy small artifacts of the lighthouses. We collected so many that we have a room in our house called the "harbor room," where photos and lighthouses convey the theme. Summer offers the opportunity to spend time finding a special addition to an already existing collection or starting a new collection. One of my sons found an interesting, large rock years ago and still has it on his bookshelf as a bookend. Collections of any kind can lead to inquiry about the topic, which moves toward finding new information from print and digital sources. The collections can be a hook for conversations and literacy activities.

These collections can also be a great way to decorate a child's room or family room with books and information surrounding the topic, which encourages further research on the subject. Special trips to the library can be planned to find more information on these topics. These collections become an important part of developing interests and hobbies. It is these interests and hobbies that motivate children to seek out information about the world. Being curious and wanting to know more about subjects are critical to developing a lifelong thirst for knowledge. When we expose children to different topics, objects, and themes, we are never certain where they might end up. In fact, collections and hobbies can take on a life of their own—short lived or lifelong. What is important here is not to worry if your child will develop an interest, but rather to do your best in exposing your child to the world. These interests grow as children acquire knowledge and enthusiasm for different subject areas. Parents who have hobbies and interests model what this lifelong pursuit is all about.

One more fun summer event is the Fourth of July. Every summer in our reading clinic, we celebrate this holiday, and children really enjoy getting ready for it. We do special activities that engage the children in learning what the holiday is all about. For families, this can be an easy opportunity to bring in related literacy activities, such as doing research on Independence Day, the history of the U.S. flag, why we celebrate with fireworks and parades, and more.

Books about the Fourth of July

- *Hats off for the Fourth of July!* by Harriet Ziefert (Viking, 2000)
- *Fourth of July Cheer* by Dee Smith (CreateSpace Independent Publishing Platform, 2015)
- *Red, White, and Boom!* by Lee Wardlaw (Henry Holt & Co., 2012)
- *The Night before the Fourth of July* by Natasha Wing (Grosset & Dunlap, 2015)

To keep the reading momentum going over the summer:

- Plan ahead for summer after the new year. Begin thinking about what summer activities your child will be engaged in.

- Before school is out, ask your child's teacher for a list of recommended summer reading books.

- Check out the public library, and see what kind of summer reading programs it offers.

- Plan a children's garden with your child.

- Check out summer programming at museums.

- Build a birdhouse or bird feeder, and hang it near a window so you can be a bird-watcher with your child. Have your child keep a record of birds sighted.

- Older children can volunteer to read to younger children or look into organizations that need volunteers to read to those in nursing homes and hospitals.

- Start collections with your children, and encourage them to seek out new information about the found objects.

Chapter Five: At-home Literacy Routines

I have created a way for people to trace their literacy development from their earliest memories of reading to today. I use this tool in my classes at the university and with in-service teachers. The questions also served as the basis for the interviews that I conducted with many parents while writing this book. I believe it is important for teachers and parents to be aware of their habits as readers in order to help children on their own quests as readers and writers. Some of the questions I ask are, "What is your recreational reading life today all about?" and "Do you read for pleasure?" The response people often give is that they just don't have enough time to read. Their lives are so busy that they just can't find the time to read for pleasure. If the goal of teaching children to read is to become lifelong readers and writers, then we need to do more to ensure that reading becomes a habit for life. One way to instill this habit is to develop daily routines for reading early on.

Do You Know Your Own Habits as a Reader?

This section is designed for you to explore your own life as a reader and begin to understand your own reading routines and habits. Let's begin with your recollection of favorite children's books. As you think about your connections to books, both past and present, think about all the experiences that have led to this point in your life. This activity allows parents, grandparents, and caregivers to trace and map backward their habits as a reader. This is especially important as we look at our literate lives and how they have evolved to this point. In some sense, this is an opportunity to examine our own individual access to books throughout our life. Access to books is an important ingredient to living literacy at home. Exploration of our own literacy development makes us aware of what habits and routines we have formed over a lifetime of reading. There is no question that the habits and routines we settle into as a family are a result of and are influenced by the way we grew up. Values are instilled early on, and families that live literacy share invaluable experiences that are hard to replicate. In some sense, it is intergenerational as we pass on our living literacy to our children and their children to come. One grandmother who I interviewed said that she married her husband "because he was a reader." She said he read novels, newspapers, and maps and generally enjoyed reading. She was sure she wanted to have children with a partner who enjoyed reading as much as she did, so they could share the experience. Clearly, being married to a reader was very important to her. She loves to read and wanted to share her life with someone who had the same zest for literacy.

A literacy life influences already established family routines. However, routines need to be evaluated periodically to see how they are working. One dad shared with me that gradually, over time, his family's after-school and evening routines had shifted, and they are not as effective as they once were. His children have after-school activities and sports practices, which get them home later in the evening. Consequently, dinner begins later and homework often seems to slide down on the priority list. It's time to reevaluate the evening routine.

In order to explore your literacy history and see how your routines might be influenced and shaped by your past and current literacy experiences, take a few minutes to reflect on the following questions.

Exploring Your Own Literacy Autobiography

To tell the story of your reading life, start with your earliest memories about books and reading. Answer the questions to reflect on all of your connections with books, before school started and through today.

- What are your earliest memories of reading?
- Do you have memories of family reading?
- How many books do you recall in your home while growing up?
- Did someone read bedtime stories to you?
  Describe these experiences as you remember them.
- What book titles and authors do you remember from growing up?
- Do you remember special places where you used to read?
- Do you have special memories about reading during the summertime?
- What do you recall about the public library while growing up?
- What do you remember about learning how to read in school? Were you in a reading group?
- What do you remember about reading in high school? Do you remember specific authors or titles?
- What are your life reading and recreational reading activities like as a reader today?
- Do you read for fun?
- About how many books have you read for recreational reading this year?

This chapter is about exploring different ways to establish routines for literacy that hopefully, over a period of time, become natural.

Developing Daily Literacy Routines

As an adult reader, I live literacy each day in my own way. Mornings are a special time for reading before the day begins. I leave reading and writing material next to my bed, so I can begin and end the day with a book or journal in my hands. It is something that I look forward to and count on as part of my routine. I can always tell when I am grumpy as it signals to me that I have not had enough time for my daily doses of literacy. I know how stressful mornings can be. There doesn't seem to be enough time to get everything done. As parents, the morning routine can be especially hectic during the school year, when there is so much to get done in what seems like not enough time. Several years ago, my niece, who was then around seven years old, woke me up in the early hours and asked me to read a story and play school with her. Beginning the day the exact way she had ended her day before amazed me. She simply needed a good night's sleep to start her literacy routines all over again. One of the most compelling interviews for this book resulted in a mother telling me about her memories with books, trips to the library, and how she and her mother lived literacy at home with daily routines. I decided to share what she told me as it is quite a moving story and touches upon the goals of this book.

"As I have been thinking more and more about growing up with books and reading in my childhood home, it has evoked so many wonderful memories. Our home was filled with books and magazines. My parents belonged to a 'book of the month' club; we had two bookshelves full of books; and although I don't remember reading any of those books, I do remember playing library and checking out those books to my dolls and invisible customers. I loved going to the library. It was so exciting to pick out books, take them home, and arrange and organize them. I got to choose several children's books, but the best was picking out the 'long' chapter book that my mother would read to me at night. I can still see those shelves with the thick, leather-bound, grown-up-looking books. One of the most memorable was *Heidi* by Johanna Spyri. My mother would climb in bed with me each night and read to me until we both fell asleep. We would be so engrossed in the lives of the characters that we would eat what they ate and feel their feelings. When thinking about *Heidi*, I can vividly remember that five-year-old orphaned girl climbing that mountain to live with her grandfather. Her aunt had layered all of the clothes she owned on her back, and she was so hot, thirsty, and tired. Then when they ate cheese and drank goat's milk, so did we. We snuggled and added blankets when winter hit the mountain and they were snowed in, and when Heidi played with the goats, my dog became a goat. I can remember begging for 'just one more' chapter. One of the other memorable books was *Little Women* by Louisa May Alcott. We felt like we knew Meg, Amy, Jo, and Beth, as they came of age during the Civil War.

We shared in their joys, triumphs, and betrayals and cried when Beth died. The other books that Mother read to me and then I reread when I was older were several series. I loved the Lucy Fitch Perkins *Twins* series. There were many that featured twins and really taught me about other cultures and countries through the lives of the twins. I remember making a cave out of sheets and furniture when we read *The Cave Twins*. It was so much fun to pretend we lived in a cave and read by the light of a flashlight. We also pretended we lived in an igloo when we read *The Eskimo Twins*. And with each different culture, we really felt what it was like to live in that country and in that time. *The Indian Twins, The Chinese Twins, The Japanese Twins*, and so many others. The other series that stands out is *The Boxcar Children*, by Gertrude Chandler Warner. I was enamored with the four orphans who created a home in a boxcar in the woods, all while keeping the secret and having wonderful adventures. We would line up the chairs to the dining room table that would become my boxcar, where I lived with my pretend siblings. Mom would let me stock the boxcar with canned goods, pots, plates, forks, and spoons. Once we drove to an appliance store where she asked for an empty refrigerator box, which we made into a boxcar. A wonderful place to read the next book."

Incorporating literacy into your daily routine doesn't have to take a lot of effort. The family calendar is something that each member should get used to checking to make sure the day is planned accordingly. Making lists of things to do before leaving for the day can help. For younger children, you might provide a whiteboard or have it posted in the kitchen and have your child check off what needs to be completed before leaving for school. This will become a habit. Gradually put the responsibility on your child to make sure tasks are completed by leaving blank list paper he or she can write on.

Things to Do Before Going to School

- Make my bed
- Have my backpack ready
- Brush my teeth
- Eat breakfast
- Take a shower
- Comb my hair

Another activity to consider is to have a copy of the newspaper on the kitchen table in the morning as a source for conversation and discussion. This is especially good for older children. Pointing out a headline and current events is a good way to start the day. Getting into the habit of reading ingredients on cereal boxes and other food containers can lead to discussions about healthy eating habits.

Bedtime Story Routines

In a recent *New York Times* article, "Bedtime Stories for Young Brains," Perri Klass, M.D. writes, "Children whose parents reported more reading at home and more books in the home showed significantly greater activation of brain areas in a region of the left hemisphere called the parietal-temporal-occipital association cortex." One of the most important gifts that a parent can give a child is the nightly bedtime story (Policastro, 2008). These special moments will add up to cherished memories that are treasured for life. The fondest memory I have of my mother from growing up was when she read to us every night from *The Child's World: Stories of Childhood*. I can still see the dress on Cinderella and Bambi's eyes from the book she read to us. I am quite certain that I ended up in this profession because of these early experiences with stories. This wonderful nightly routine can foster a lifetime love of reading. With my own sons, reading nightly was something they looked forward to each day. Very often, they would ask for the same story to be read. We read both fiction and nonfiction selections that were derived from their interests.

There are several ways to share bedtime stories. You can read stories and informational text together, you can tell stories that are made up or real, you can transmit stories from your own life, you can share family history, you can write stories, and you can sing songs or act out stories together.

Why Tell Stories?

The reasons for telling stories go well beyond entertainment. Stories are used to convey social messages and solve real-world problems. Historically, the story was used to preserve the culture of a civilization. Often the only records of a society were the oral stories passed down from generation to generation. As time went on, stories were also used as a means of instructing others (Stein & Policastro, 1984). Thus, there are many purposes and many different types of stories: sad stories, happy ending stories, humiliating stories, scary stories, instructional stories, consolatory stories, guilt-inducing stories, and more. Stories have unlimited possibilities as "the only constraints placed upon the content and function of stories originate in the teller" (Stein & Policastro, 1984). Consequently, stories are a device to help us understand our world and make meaning out of life.

Weaving storytelling into our daily routines can be an easy habit to establish. Although before bedtime is the perfect time and a time to count on each evening, other times during the day work as well, such as while driving in the car, getting a meal ready, or standing in line at the grocery store.

Learning Story and Narrative Structure

When children are listening to stories, reading stories, acting out stories, or writing stories, they are learning the important elements of a story. Narrative structure or story structure has certain components that, when learned and understood, assist in overall comprehension of the text. Learning the structures within a story will enhance the literacy lessons children encounter in school. Literacy lessons are all about comprehension of text, and at least 50 percent of instruction in most early elementary classrooms focuses on narrative text. The more a child is exposed to stories within the home, the more these narrative structural elements will be internalized by the listener. The following are some of the elements that children learn when stories are integrated into their literacy life:

- Stories have a beginning, a middle, and an end.

- Stories have a sequence of events that are in order of the action.

- Stories take place during a time period that could be long ago, today, or in the future.

- Stories have a setting and take place somewhere in the world or out of this world (e.g., fantasy).

- Stories have characters that can be people, animals, or other creatures.

- Stories have a theme or a goal that the characters are trying to achieve or strive for.

- Stories have characters that try to solve problems in order to meet their goal or quest.

- Stories have characters that have emotional reactions to all the events in the story.

- Stories have endings or resolutions to the problems that the characters endure.

Family Stories

Telling family stories is a terrific way to share and preserve your family history. These stories help children understand their past and make meaning from their present life. My parents shared stories of growing up during the war and how times were challenging. They shared stories with a sense of hope and prosperity, never with doom or despair. My father was in the army during World War II and my children were quite interested in all aspects of his war stories. He would tell details of what it was like to be in the army, and he shared important artifacts with them, such as his uniform, mementos from places he had traveled, his military badges and pins, and pictures of himself with other soldiers. My children learned important history pertaining to the war straight from a soldier who was on the ground fighting for our country. These stories were told and retold to my children as they could never get enough of grandpa's army stories. This is a treasured memory for me as I heard many of these stories for the first time, too. I know my children will hold those stories close and share them with their own children.

In the example shown here, my son wrote and illustrated a five-sentence story titled "The War." It was a story that clearly indicated how he internalized his grandpa's war stories. My son's hours and hours of playing with tiny green army soldiers on the playroom floor also helped him develop an internal narrative for the story. Although rudimentary in nature, it has a beginning, a middle, and an end. The illustrations are key and highlight the setting and place along with characters and action. I'm convinced that his story was influenced by both listening to family stories and conducting his own dramatic play.

Stories you tell to your own children can include what you remember from growing up, along with stories your parents and grandparents may have shared.

You can also share information about your heritage and culture. My mother's parents were born in Poland, and I know very little about them. They died when my mother was quite young, so the transmission of the oral family history was broken. Some possible story starters for transmitting your family story could include:

- Share what you know and remember about your grandparents' lives growing up, including where they were born and raised.
- Talk about where you were born and raised.
- Tell a story about your first day of school and other school-related experiences.
- Share a story about how you celebrated holidays growing up.
- Tell about a special day that is dear to you from growing up.
- Tell about a special birthday that you celebrated when you were young.
- Tell about your first time learning how to ride a bike or swim.
- Tell stories over time about your life growing up, and include how you have gotten to where you are now.
- Use pictures and artifacts to begin a story or to add details about an event.

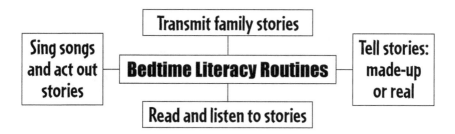

Telling Stories Made-up and Real

We had a bedtime story that lasted a span of 15 years. It all started one night after I read a story aloud to my sons and turned off the light. I said "Once upon a time, there was a mommy fish, a daddy fish, and a baby fish. They were all happy living in the beautiful ocean." Each night, I would add a scene about the life of the family of fish, and I never knew ahead of time exactly what would happen next. The events that took place always included a challenge or a problem that the fish encountered and needed to overcome. Over time, this story took many twists and turns as they went on picnics, vacations, and other adventures but always faced a challenge of some sort (storm rolling in before the picnic, baby fish getting lost on vacation). I always made sure that there was a hopeful conclusion to the episode before my sons went to sleep (storm passed quickly and they were able to have the picnic; the baby fish was just hiding behind a rock, was found easily, and the vacation resumed as planned). My children asked for this fish story every night and thought that I had an ending. They would ask me about it during the day and wanted to know more about what was going to happen next. I would always keep them in suspense by telling them it would continue at bedtime. This routine was something they looked forward to, and they would hurry through bath time in order to hear more of the story. My sons' friends would spend the night and couldn't wait to hear about what happened since the last time they were over and heard the story. What was so interesting and unexpected for me was that the fish story influenced their writing and dictating of stories when they were in school. The example below shows how my son clearly used the bedtime story as his structure for the story he dictated.

The Killer whale was coming to eat a shark and some pirates came and they tried to Kill the Killer whale and the shark. The Captain said "Break it up." Then a whale came. He tipped the pirate ship over. The pirates

1.

threw their swords at the Killer whale. Then some soldiers came on a small boat. Then a baby Killer whale came. He tipped the soldiers' boat over. Then a pirate whale came. He started fighting with all the people. Then a nice whale came and all the people got on his back.

The End

2.

Aaron Shepard's Home Page:

Stories, Scripts, and More: This site has free resources for storytelling that include an online guide, articles, and recommended readings.

I interviewed many parents to not only hear about their current parenting and literacy experiences, but how they had grown up with literacy. One mother I interviewed grew up in Mexico, and she recalled how during the summer she would go to her grandmother's farm. This farm had no electricity, so when it got dark out, they would roast pumpkin seeds on the fire and her grandmother would tell scary stories. There were no books in her grandmother's house or in her house when she was growing up. Rather, stories were told at bedtime. Another mother I interviewed is Assyrian and also did not have any books in her home while growing up in London. However, her parents told stories as well. She recalled her father telling her the story of "Tom Thumb," a character tied to English folklore. She remembered her mother talking about life back home in Iraq, the war going on, and all the struggles they had to endure. Her mother was able to weave stories about her life into teaching an appreciation for life. Today, these parents are avid readers and spend a great deal of time reading to their children.

Reading Bedtime Stories

Because my mother read to me and my siblings every night, it became a natural habit for me to read to my children. I started reading to them when they were born and had books surrounding them in their cribs, at bath time, and more. Reading a bedtime story can begin at a very early age and continue for many years. Starting this routine early on establishes a special time each day to look forward to. There are many ways to begin a bedtime story routine. You will need to see what works best for your family situation and your life. Something that worked especially well for our family was to count on the bedtime story after baths were completed and children were ready for bed. For some reason, this always had a calming effect on the children. By starting gradually, the bedtime story can become a family habit. One important factor is to be sure to turn off the TV and remove any other distractions.

Both fiction and nonfiction informational texts are good choices for reading selections. Exposing children to a variety of genres provides a way for them to experience a wide range of texts. What you read at bedtime does not need to always be the same. You can bring in newspaper and magazine articles or informational books. Some favorites in our family were books by Richard Scarry and David Macaulay. These authors wrote about objects and how things work in the world. For young children, talk about choices and reading preferences, such as stories about animals, make believe, mysteries, and adventures. Wordless picture books can be a great way for you both to share the story by pointing to the pictures and asking prediction questions.

Five Tips for Reading Aloud to Your Child

1. Be interested in and excited about the book or materials you read with your child.

2. Select fiction and nonfiction stories and informational text that includes content about the world, nature, science, and other topics of interest to your child.

3. Use different voices and change volume when you read so that your child learns about what reading with expression sounds like. Whisper for a soft message, and raise your voice for a loud thought. Read as if you are the character and be as animated as possible. Use facial and vocal expressions. Exaggerate your speech when appropriate. Use props for extra fun.

4. Keep the book wide open when you read so your child can see all the illustrations. Point out the title, author, and illustrator on the book's front cover. Stop and talk about the illustrations on the cover and on each page.

5. Highlight words as you read. Stop and talk about an interesting word and use it in context for your child to understand the meaning.

Tips and Suggestions for Establishing the Bedtime Story Routine

Reading every night is an important goal in establishing strong home-school partnerships. Just imagine if you read every night to your child for a year: that would be 365 literacy encounters. Here are a few tips for the nightly routine.

- Start with classics and favorites, and go back to them whenever you want. It is fine to read a book over and over. Children love repeated readings and never seem to tire of the old favorites like *Goodnight Moon* by Margaret Wise Brown.

- Be sure to point out the author and illustrator, and make a big deal about the front cover of the book.

- Read every night. Establish a routine by reading at the same time each evening. Always turn off the TV and limit other distractions.

- Make a bookmark with your child that is just for bedtime reading. Write on the bookmark to keep track of stories read. Write "What do you think is going to happen next in the story?" on the bookmark as a reminder to ask this important question.

- Mix up the reading materials and include nonfiction informational texts.

- Ask simple prediction questions as you read, such as "How do you think the characters will solve the problem?"

- Keep books near the bed, and establish a bedtime story shelf or nook.

- Keep favorite books under the pillow for easy access.

Sing Songs, Act Out Stories, and Pretend Play

In some cultures, singing songs is an important part of the bedtime routine. Singing songs can be a nice way to have fun with your child before bedtime. Traditional songs, play rhymes, and nursery rhymes work well. Hansen and Bernstorf (2002) make the connection between music and literacy development. Songs work especially well when you are transitioning from one routine to another, such as after dinner or homework to bath time. Just about all of the nursery rhymes and finger play rhymes use a similar form. Teaching your child the song first makes it very easy for them to then read the words in print. You can download these songs and listen and sing along together. One particular song that resonates with me is "Take Me out to the Ballgame." I'm pretty sure we sang this song no fewer than several hundred times in our house. When I hear it at baseball games and I'm with my sons, we just smile and laugh, remembering all the times we sang it as a family. Children love to sing songs and develop favorites quickly. An important aspect of singing songs with young children is developing their awareness of the sounds that letters make, including rhyming. **Phonemic awareness** is a critical prerequisite skill needed for decoding words in print. When children hear the sounds and have lots of practice with them, it is easier for them to sound out words while reading.

Here are some classic songs to listen to and print out the words for reading and singing.

"London Bridge Is Falling Down"

"Old MacDonald Had a Farm"

"Row, Row, Row Your Boat"

"The Alphabet Song"

"The Farmer in the Dell"

"The Itsy Bitsy Spider"

"Twinkle, Twinkle, Little Star"

"Yankee Doodle"

> ### Raffi Songs to Read Series
>
> *(Crown Books for Young Readers)*
> *Baby Beluga*
> *Down by the Bay*
> *Shake My Sillies Out*
> *Wheels on the Bus*

Acting out stories is also a lot of fun for children. One of my sons pretended he was Superman for at least a year. And his best friend who lived next door pretended he was Batman. In the summer and on weekends, my son would wake up in his Superman pajamas and keep them on all day. His friend would come over in his Batman costume, and they would play the entire day, acting out different scenarios. Pretending to be superheroes was not only fun and entertaining, but allowed them to imagine what it was like to have a super power, using creativity to the maximum. My son devoured Superman comics, watched Superman movies, and read anything he could find about other superheroes. Another son played "Army" with his army men for hours on end. The entire playroom floor would be set up as intricate battlefields. I would notice that he would be having conversations with himself, talking to pretend officers. His pretend play included lots of thinking and work as he would often fall asleep right in the middle of the floor. He watched movies and sought out children's books about the military and combat. He loved reading, writing about, listening to, and seeking out any and all information on soldiers.

We have one student in our Summer Reading Clinic who, for the past two years, has arrived dressed as a princess. We all await her arrival to see what she will be wearing. On the parent information sheet, we ask "What types of books does your child like?" This student's parent's response was "Loves princesses."

Drama as play and acting out stories is another way to develop the bedtime routine. Dramatic play or pretend play is a way of representing the story or narrative. Pretend or dramatic play can be based on a made-up story or a spin-off from an existing story. This is a wonderful opportunity for parents to capitalize on using costumes, toys, props, and other household items to bring a story to life. Puppets are another way to add some fun when reading and acting out stories.

In one kindergarten classroom, the teacher had just read a book to the students about the alphabet and came to the letter "I" for "imagination." She asked the students what that word meant. They had a discussion about pretending, make-believe, and dressing up in costumes. One girl said that she has a mirror at home and lots of dresses in which she pretends she is different Disney characters. Another little boy raised his hand and said that he dresses up as Woody, Buzz Lightyear, Batman, and Spiderman. The children all talked about how they like to pretend being other characters. Pretending is a critical dimension to language and literacy development because it takes children out of the here and now and allows them to use their imagination. Imagination is necessary for both reading and writing. When children read, they must be able to imagine the story and information as it unfolds. This is true for both fiction and nonfiction text. If you are reading a story, you need to imagine where the story takes place and what the characters are like. If you are reading informational text about how wind farms work, for example, you need to be able to imagine it in action. Using props and costumes helps children make meaning and bring life to what they are pretending. Imagination and creativity should be recognized as an important part of daily play. You can encourage pretend play by doing the following:

- Keep a box of props—hats, bags, accessories, and other dress-up items—so your child can act out and pretend play.

- Make puppets from socks and small brown paper bags to have fun with when reading, making up stories, and acting out stories.

- Make a flannel/felt board, and cut out characters and scene pieces to align with stories you have read and made up.

- Have your child retell stories you have read and listened to.

Model Reading and Writing Daily

Modeling reading books and other print materials, especially with young children, is something parents should strive to do on a daily basis. Children need role models to form habits and routines. When we model reading and writing, we are showing children that we value literacy and that it is important in our own lives.

Modeling reading and writing for different purposes is important as children need to know that we read for pleasure, work, and many other reasons that help us succeed in a print and digital society. Children also need to see parents reading all types of print and for different periods of time, depending on the purpose.

Here are some tips for modeling reading and writing:

- Let your child catch you reading and writing often.

- Make a deliberate choice to read for extended periods of time, so your child can see sustained reading in action (this is what good readers do).

- Use free time or make time to read on long car, plane, bus, or train rides.

- Talk to your child about the latest book you are reading.

- If you work, talk to your child about what you need to read and write for work.

Setting up a Homework Routine

Chapter Three outlines many ways in which families can set up a homework center. Embedded in the idea of a homework center is a scheduled routine. For younger children, the routine needs to be established early on in the primary grades and evaluated every so often to take into account other after-school activities. By building the routine over time, children will make it a habit that is practiced independently. As children move up through the grades, this routine will need to be adjusted to meet the demands of different kinds of homework. Routines take time to establish. And sticking to a homework routine might have its challenges along the way, so the routine will need to be firm yet flexible to meet each family's changing needs. Here are some tips for establishing homework routines:

- Be specific with your homework routine by starting it at a certain time each day.

- Start the routine with an after-school snack and conversation.

- Have the time for homework blocked out on your family calendar.

- Transition into the homework by unpacking the backpack and taking out what needs to get completed, including supplies.

- Organize the work area.

- If you miss a routine one day, start again the next day.

- After weekends and vacations, recognize that it might take a bit of time to get back into the routine.

Weekend and Summer Routines That Include Literacy-rich Experiences

Chapter Four goes into detail about using weekends and summers as a time to engage in literacy activities for the entire family. Making these activities a routine is the next natural step. Plan weekend events together during the week, and talk about the activities that you will be engaged in to build excitement. Do the same for summer during the spring so your child can begin to plan ahead.

- Make a weekend day a literacy-rich day with planned activities and outings.

- Write down outings on the family calendar, and block out time each week so family members can plan ahead and anticipate the outing.

Make Visiting the Library a Routine

One mother I interviewed for this book told me that her daughter would cry when it was time to leave the library on Saturday morning. Often they would stay for at least an hour and a half. She was embarrassed when her daughter would cry and not want to leave. I assured her that this was something that should not cause embarrassment. In fact, she should be pleased that her daughter loves the library so much that she doesn't want to leave. She is providing a gift for her daughter: a library routine established early. This mother established a routine with her daughter. They would talk about how many books she would check out and bring home. During the week, they would read the books and discuss them together. When I talked to her, they were checking out up to seven books at a time.

When I travel for both business and pleasure, I often make it a point to visit the public library in the city I'm in. On a recent trip to a large urban city, I was struck by how many teenagers were in the teen section of the library during the summer. There were teens reading independently all around, there was a small group working on computers, and there were several teens who were playing video games.

Important here is that these teens had established a routine for summer reading in the library. They were not there with parents. Rather, they came on their own. Here are some tips for establishing a library routine:

- Set a weekly schedule to visit the public library.

- Make a special place in your home just for library books.

- For older children and teens, let them choose their own books.

- Check out the Young Adult Library Services Association's "Teens' Top 10," which includes the best books of the year for young adults.

- Take time to read and talk about books checked out of the library.

- Talk about new books that you hope to check out.

- Use the library website to reserve books, check out new books that have arrived, view special events, and more.

- Be sure to check out the summer reading programs in your library for young children and teens.

Final Thoughts

I hope you enjoyed reading this book as much as I have enjoyed writing it. It has been a pure joy to write, allowing me to weave memories of my own childhood and literacy with memories of raising my four sons to be readers with the career-wide experiences of working with children and parents who want to raise lifelong readers and writers. My love of books and libraries is who I am as a person, parent, and educator. While writing this book, my oldest son was making preparations to propose to his girlfriend. We knew he was considering a spot in New York but didn't know the exact location, date, or details. In fact, we thought it would probably be in upstate New York where he was planning a ski trip with his college buddies. Just as this book was going to the printer, he surprised us and got engaged in the Fordham University library (the 4th floor where he used to study with his girlfriend) while on his way to the ski trip. The thought of him getting engaged in a library never, ever crossed my mind as a possibility. I share this story as an example of how living literacy can play out in the lives of our children.

Family experiences, conversations, reading to and with your children, and much more all contribute to shaping literacy development. No matter where you live, every day can provide fun, joyful, and literacy-rich opportunities for you and your children. It is my hope that every home is living literacy.

References

Adams, P. (2015). Extra: Parental involvement contributes to better grades, attendance and graduation rates. *Journal Start,* July 22, 2015.

Allington, R. L. & McGill-Franzen, A. (Eds.). (2013). *Summer reading: Closing the rich/poor reading achievement gap.* NY: Teachers College Press.

Barone, D. (2015). The fluid nature of literacy: A look at how the definition of literacy has changed and what it means for today's students. *Literacy Today,* 33(1).

Barrentine, S. J. (1996). Engaging with interactive read-alouds. *The Reading Teacher,* 50: 36–43.

Bauman, J. F. & Graves, M. F. (2010). What is academic vocabulary? *Journal of Adolescent and Adult Literacy.* 54: 4–12.

Carter, D. R., Chard, D. J. & Pool, J. L. (2009). A family strengthens approach to early language and literacy development. *Early Childhood Education Journal,* 36: 519–526.

Cohen, V. L. & Cowen, J. E. (2011). *Literacy for children in an information age: Teaching reading, writing and thinking.* 2nd Edition. Belmont, CA: Wadsworth.

Council of Chief State School Officers & National Governors Association Center for Best Practices (2015). *Common Core State Standards Initiative: About the Standards.* Washington, DC: Council of Chief State School Officers.

Craig-Post, M. (2015). Literacy starts at home: Family engagement is imperative for continued student achievement. *Reading Today,* 32(6): 8–9.

Daniels, H. (2004). Building a classroom library. *National Council of Teachers of English,* 11: 44–45.

Duke, N. (2003). Beyond once upon a time. *Instructor,* November/December.

Fitzgerald, J. (1999, October). What is this thing called "balance"? *The Reading Teacher,* 53(2): 100–106.

Ford, M. P. & Opitz, M. F. (2011). Looking back to move forward with guided reading. *Reading Horizons:* 225–240.

Fountas, I. C. & Pinnell, G. S. (1996). *Guided reading: Good first teaching for all children.* Portsmouth, NH: Heinemann.

Frey, B. B., Lee, S. W., Tollefson, N., Pass, L. & Massengill, D. (2005). Balanced literacy in an urban school district. *Journal of Educational Research,* 98(5): 272–280.

Gill, S. R. (2006). Teaching rimes with shared reading. *The Reading Teacher:* 191–193.

Goldstein, D. (2015). Don't help your kids with their homework and other insights from ground-breaking study of how parents impact children's academic achievement. *Atlantic Monthly*, April 2014. Retrieved December 28, 2015, from http://www.theatlantic.com/magazine/archive/2014/04/and-dont-help-your-kids-with-their-homework/358636/.

Goodman, K. (2015). *Dear Mr. Huey: Here's what we've learned in the last century about literacy*. Paper presented at the International Literacy Association Conference, St. Louis, MO.

Greene, W. P., Magarity, D. & Toth, R. (1998). *Museums and learning: A guide for family visits*. U.S. Department of Education, Office of Educational Research and Improvement.

Hansen, D. & Bernstorf, E. (2002). Linking music learning to reading instruction. *Music Education Journal*, 88(5), 17–21, 52.

Harris, T. & Hodges, R. E. (1995). *The literacy dictionary*. Newark, DE: International Reading Association.

Harste, J., Woodward, V. & Burke, C. (1984). *Language stories and literacy lessons*. Portsmouth, NH: Heinemann.

Kendall, J. (2011). *Understanding Common Core State Standards*. Alexandria, VA: ASCD.

Klass, P. (2015). Bedtime stories for young brains. *New York Times*. Retrieved August 17, 2015, from http://well.blogs.nytimes.com/2015/08/17/bedtime-stories-for-young-brains/?_r=0.

Kletzien, S. B. (1992). Reading workshop: Reading, writing, thinking. *Journal of Reading*, 35: 444–451.

Kotaman, H. (2013). Impacts of dialogical storybook reading on young children's reading attitude and vocabulary development. *Reading Improvement*, 45(2): 199–205

Lilly, E. & Green, C. (2004). *Developing partnerships with families through children's literature*. Upper Saddle River, NJ: Pearson/Merrill Prentice Hall.

Lindsey, J. (2013). Interventions that increase children's access to print material and improve their reading proficiencies. R. L. Allington & A. McGill-Franzen, (Eds.). *Summer reading: Closing the rich/poor reading achievement gap* (pp. 20–38). NY: Teachers College Press and Newark, DE: International Reading Association.

Martinez, M. (2006). What is metacognition? *Phi Delta Kappan*, 87: 4.

Moser, L. (2015) Congress is close to replacing No Child Left Behind. So what will change? *Slate*. Retrieved December 28, 2015, from http://www.slate.com/blogs/schooled/2015/11/18/esea_bill_getting_close_to_passage_in_congress_what_will_change_once_no.html.

Ohlhausen, M. M. & Jepsen, M. (1992). Lessons from Goldilocks: "Somebody's been choosing my books but I can make my own choices now!" *New Advocate*, 5(1), 31–46.

Paulsen, G. (2000). *Hatchet*. NY: Simon & Schuster Books for Young Readers.

Policastro, M. M. (1985). What's happening: Predicting before, during, and after the picture. *The Reading Teacher*, 38(9): 60–65.

Policastro, M. M. (2008). *The bedtime story*. Reach Out and Read Newsletter of the American Academy of Pediatrics.

Policastro, M. M., Mazeski, D. & McTague, B. (2010–2011). Creating parent libraries: Enhancing family literacy through access to books. *Illinois Reading Council Journal*, 39(1).

Policastro, M. M., McTague, B. & Mazeski, D. (2016). *Formative assessment in the new balanced literacy classroom*. North Mankato, MN: Capstone.

Policastro, M. M. & McTague, B. (2015). *The new balanced literacy school: Implementing Common Core*. North Mankato, MN: Capstone.

Powell, D. R. & D'Angelo, D. (2000). *Guide to improving parenting education in Even Start family literacy programs*. Washington, DC: U.S. Department of Education.

Randall, K. (2002). High stakes testing: What is at stake? *American Annals of the Deaf*. 145: 390–393.

Read Aloud 15 Minutes (n.d.). *Read Aloud 15*. Retrieved November 10, 2015, from http://readaloud.org.

Reading Rockets (2010). *Environmental print*. Retrieved November 1, 2015, from www.ReadingRockets.org.

Reese, E., Sparks, A. & Leyva, D. (2010). A review of parent interventions for preschool children's language and emergent literacy. *Journal of Early Childhood Literacy*, 10(1) 97–117.

Rogers, K. *Selecting just the right book for your child to read*. Retrieved September 2015 from www.readingtogether.org.

Ruth, N. (2014). All of the above: Turning the page on close reading. *California English*, Nov. 2014.

Seel, N. (2012). Phonological awareness. *Encyclopedia of the Sciences of Learning*.

Spiegel, D. L. (1998). Silver bullets, babies, and bath water. *The Reading Teacher*, 52(2): 114–124.

Stein, N. L. & Policastro, M. M. (1984). The concept of a story: A comparison between children's and teachers' viewpoints in H. Manol, N. Stein, and T. Trabasso (Eds.) *Learning and Comprehension of Text*. Hillsdale, NJ: Lawrence Erlbaum Associates.

Teale, W. H. & Sulzby, E. (1989). *Emergent literacy: New perspectives.* In D. S. Strickland & L. M. Morrow (Eds.) *Emergent literacy: Young children learn to read and write*. Newark, DE: International Reading Association.

Tompkins, G. E. (2013). *Literacy for the 21st century: Teaching reading and writing in prekindergarten through grade 4*. Upper Saddle River, NJ: Pearson/Merrill Prentice Hall.

UNESCO (2006). *Education for all: A global monitoring report*. Paris, France: UNESCO.

U.S. Department of Education, National Center for Education Statistics (2013). *The Nation's Report Card: A First Look: 2013 Mathematics and Reading* (NCES 2014–451). Washington, DC: U.S. Government Printing Office. Retrieved July 8, 2015, from http://nces.ed.gov/ nationsreportcard/pubs/main2013/2014451.aspx.

U.S. Department of Education, Office of Intergovernmental and Interagency Affairs, Educational Partnerships and Family Involvement Unit (2003). *Homework tips for parents*. Washington, DC: U.S. Department of Education.

Webster-Smith, M. (2010). Literacy memories, definitions, implications. *Language Arts Journal of Michigan*, 26(1): 16–17.

Appendix

Simple and Fun Daily Activities

1. Sports: Attend or watch games on TV or listen to them together on the radio. Try attending a sporting event and learning something new with your child. Sporting events are perfect for follow-up activities, including more reading and writing about the event, making a book, or keeping a scrapbook of artifacts collected. Research the different histories and heroes of sports. Read biographies and autobiographies about sports heroes. Read the newspaper sports section, and check out sports magazines at the library or subscribe to them.

2. Entertainment: Check out community theater events for families and children. See a play, puppet show, concert, or musical. Read the book and then watch the movie or ballet and discuss with your child which one you liked better with detail, evidence, and comparisons. Write about the event, including a review of the performance.

3. Travel and Recreation: Plan a vacation, and let your child help make decisions and choices. Get travel information and brochures, and spend time reading and having conversations about the destination. Look at maps and study the area of the destination. Plan your vacation around special family events at your destination. Talk about your modes of transportation (air, car, train, or boat). Have fun looking into different options and daily schedules for your trip.

4. Household Chores: Teach children early on about taking responsibility for household chores. Make lists of chores for your child to accomplish, and teach him or her related words as you go: vacuum, dust, mop, make your bed, laundry sorting, and folding. Let your child add chores to the list. Be sure to make a list of the cleaning supplies you will need to accomplish the chores.

5. Turn Your Favorite Book into a Game: For suggestions, check out the book *Journey to Game Land: How to Make a Board Game from Your Favorite Children's Book* by Ben Buchanan, Carol Adams, and Susan Allison.

6. Frequent the Library: Make a big deal out of going to the public library and especially getting a library card for your child. Set aside time each week for the library visit and make sure it goes on your family calendar. When traveling and on vacation, stop by the local library. Many public libraries are charming places to visit and photograph.

7. Nature: Take advantage of the outdoors and utilize every aspect as a literacy opportunity. Follow the seasons of the year and use nature as a springboard for authentic learning. Explore the outdoors and model inquiry questions for your child, such as "Where does a rain drop come from?" Use these experiences to align with books about nature and the natural world.

8. Family Game Night: Set aside a night to have fun playing games with your family. Let your child know that this is a special time to have fun. Make the learning indirect.

9. Drawing and Art: Use drawing and other art activities to promote literacy. Have your child draw a picture of an event, an experience, or something he or she wants. This is a good way to encourage creativity. Use drawing and art with writing, and add illustrations to the text. When reading a story, keep a dry-erase whiteboard close by so you can ask your child to draw the answer to questions, such as "What do you think is going to happen next in the story?"

10. Go on a Reading Picnic: Pack your lunch, add some books, and head outdoors for a reading picnic. Use this time to read aloud or read to yourself while your child reads.

11. Tents and Forts: Rainy days are a perfect time to get out all the blankets and sheets and let your child make a tent or fort in the house. Bring a flashlight and books inside for a fun place to read.

12. Celebrations: Celebrations are something that families should document through photos, scrapbooking, journals, and more. Celebrations can be both small and big and elicit many different kinds of literacy activities, including through social media.

13. Family Calendar: Keep a large family calendar in the kitchen or family room as documentation and a planner for all family events. Refer to it often and have conversations about upcoming events. Encourage your child to add events to the calendar, check off completed events, and more.

14. Scrapbook: This is a great way to document experiences with your family using photographs and other artifacts, collections, and more. Have your child write about the experience and add it to the scrapbook. Create a space in your home for this special activity, and make it an ongoing and authentic part of your family.

15. Puzzles: Utilize the crossword puzzle in the newspaper daily. Engage the entire family in solving the word puzzles together. Leave it out on the kitchen counter with a note to "Take a turn."

16. Love and Label Your Environment: Label a few objects in your environment to help your child learn new words. Some examples might include "mirror," "bathtub," and "shower" in your bathroom. Have fun with the words, and give your child time to learn the words before adding more. Two or three words at a time are just fine.

17. Build a List of Favorite Books: Begin a list of favorite books read by family members and add to it. Keep this list where everyone can see it and contribute to it. Talk about the books as you are reading them.

18. Humor: Read funny stories and laugh. Post a joke or riddle of the day in the kitchen.

19. Comic Books and Comics: Don't forget to include comic books as another way to engage your child in a variety of types of reading pleasure. Comics are fun and tell a story, and your child will infer through context and pictures. Include classics like Archie and Spiderman. Check out the comics in the newspaper as well.

20. Collections: Collect objects and artifacts of interest. These can start with a trip, a visit to a museum, or just a walk along the beach. Collections can turn into hobbies and be a terrific way for children to inquire about the objects.

21. Start a Neighborhood Book Club for Kids: A neighborhood book club can be for both young children as well as for older children and teens. Younger children will need the organization and structure to decide what to read and where to meet. Older children can manage this by themselves and make decisions about what to read.

22. Get a Globe: Place your globe in a space where there is easy access for the family to explore. Help your child learn geography by pointing out the countries in the world. Extend the activities to a map.

23. Swap Books: Start a program, like a Little Free Library, in your neighborhood, church, school, or other places where you and your family have read a book or where you can exchange books. These can function with little management.

24. Read to Your Pet: If you have a pet, this can be a great way to encourage your child to read. Reading to a dog, cat, or fish can give your child an opportunity to read aloud for fun and use expression without having to worry about reading every word correctly. The purpose of this activity is fun, but it also builds confidence by reading aloud.

25. Buy Books as Presents: Every time you or your child needs a gift, think of buying a book as the present. Holidays, birthdays, and other celebrations are the perfect way to show your child that reading is so important that you give books to others as gifts.

Online Literacy Resources

ABC Teach: Free printable activities for kids.

American Library Association: Great resource for checking out award-winning books like Caldecott Medal and Newbery Medal winners.

Between the Lions: Get Wild about Reading: Companion site for the PBS television series that includes more than 70 illustrated online stories, activities, interactive games, printable text, and much more.

Boys Read: An organization of parents, educators, and librarians whose mission is to transform boys into lifelong readers.

BrainPOP: Animated curriculum content that engages students.

Carol Hurst's Children's Literature Site: Resources for both home and school that include books for children and activities for using them.

Center for Parenting Education: Offers parenting support by building off of families' strengths so that children thrive academically, socially, and behaviorally.

Children's Book Council: An organization dedicated to promoting and encouraging the enjoyment of children's books. You can find resources about authors and illustrators and information on National Children's Book Week.

Cooperative Children's Book Center (CCBC): A link to 50 multicultural books every child should know.

Family Education: Resources, quizzes, games, after-school activities, and much more.

Fun English Games for Kids: Great resource for learning English that includes games, activities, videos, and more.

Imagination Soup: Features comics, games, graphic novels, information about authors, and more.

International Literacy Association: Professional organization (formerly the International Reading Association) that announces Children's Choices books (100 titles), Teachers' Choices books (30 titles), and Young Adults' Choices books (30 titles).

Kids Comics: Helps you find a kid-friendly comic book store in your area; features new comics, upcoming comics, and links to graphic novels.

Multicultural Children's Literature: Covers multicultural literature and summarizes the books in an annotated bibliography.

National Association for the Education of Young Children (NAEYC): A professional organization promoting high-quality learning for all children from birth through age eight by connecting policy, practice, and research.

National Center for Families Learning (NCFL): Works to strengthen and broaden approaches to family literacy, building on advancements in education and technology as well as the changing needs of families.

National Summer Learning Association: Provides resources, guidance, and expertise to the summer learning community.

New York Public Library Digital Collection: Includes a database of more than 600,000 images from art, humanities, sciences, performing arts, and more. The collection includes podcasts, videos, animated talking books, and much more.

Parent Teacher Association (PTA): This association provides information to help families get involved in their child's school. Also includes many other issues relevant to today and raising children.

Reading Is Fundamental (RIF): Organization that provides free books and literacy resources with the mission of motivating children to read by working with parents and the community. Site includes extensive resources for parents, including booklets, articles, brochures, and multicultural resources.

Smithsonian Virtual Field Trip: Take a panoramic, room-by-room, virtual tour of the Smithsonian Museum.

Succeed to Read: Resources for parents and teachers on teaching reading.

The Idea Box: Community-driven website that provides literacy activities that can be done at home with your child.

TOPICS Online Magazine for Learners of English: An online magazine where English language learners can participate and express opinions and ideas on topics of interest. Students share with others who are learning English.

White House Virtual Tour: An up-close and personal look at one of the most famous places in the world. You can click on any room that you want to visit.

Glossary of Literacy Terms

Balanced literacy: A philosophical perspective that shows reading and writing success are developed through different methods of instruction, varying by level of teacher support and child control. There is no one correct way a teacher can teach reading to a student, but rather a balanced technique to create literacy growth (Policastro & McTague, 2015).

Benchmark assessment: Assessments given at several points during the academic year. The purpose of administering a benchmark assessment is to establish baseline data or levels of achievement data and track and measure progress toward learning standards or goals.

Classroom library: A place in the classroom where all types of fiction and nonfiction, books, magazines, clippings, articles, brochures, and newspapers are organized. Some of this material will pertain directly to the subjects children study in school (literature, history, science, mathematics) while other parts of the collection can be random, chosen merely because they interest many, some, or just a few young readers (Daniels, 2004).

Close reading: A personal or instructional routine that involves studying a text by deliberately rereading it. The purpose of close reading is three-fold: to better understand a text's meaning through how it was written (organization, choice of words, style, choice of key details, and arguments); to find out the author's purpose; and to discover the way in which the text informs, entertains, or presents an argument to the reader (Ruth, 2014).

Common Core State Standards: A set of high-quality academic standards in mathematics and English language arts/literacy (ELA). These learning goals frame what a student should know and be able to do at the end of each grade. The standards were formed to ensure that all students graduate from high school with the skills and knowledge essential to succeed in college, career, and life, regardless of where they live (Council of Chief State School Officers & National Governors Association Center for Best Practices, 2015).

Emergent literacy: Reading and writing behaviors that precede and develop into conventional literacy. It is concerned with the earliest phases of development between birth and when children read and write conventionally (Teale & Sulzby, 1989).

Environmental print: The print of everyday life that appears all around us in logos, labels, street signs, food wrappers, store names, and much more (Reading Rockets, 2010).

Formative assessment: A range of formal and informal assessments used to modify teaching and learning activities to best achieve student success (Policastro, McTague & Mazeski, 2016).

Guided reading: Planned, intentional, focused reading instruction during which the teacher helps students learn more about the reading process. This is usually done in small groups with a book chosen by the teacher (Ford & Opitz, 2011).

High-stakes assessments: Statewide testing programs to determine if students are meeting the state standards and benchmarks before leaving the public school system or moving onto another grade (Randall, 2002).

Independent reading and writing: Part of the classroom literacy routine where students have an opportunity to read and write independently, including in all content areas (Policastro & McTague, 2015).

Informational text: Nonfiction, factual text that enables the reader to learn about the world, including the natural and social world. The purpose of informational texts is to present facts, various forms of content, and concepts (Duke, 2003).

Interactive read-aloud: This session of reading a book out loud encourages children to engage in dialogue and discourse through answering questions posed by the teacher. The children interact with each other as they seek to construct meaning (Barrentine, 1996).

Literacy: The basic ability to read and write and use those skills in everyday life scenarios (Webster-Smith, 2010).

Literacy block: A guide for setting up a classroom routine that could include time for read-alouds, small groups, guided reading instruction, language and literacy centers, and independent reading and writing (Policastro & McTague, 2015).

Metacognition: Monitoring and control of one's own thought (Martinez, 2006).

Multimodal literacy: A theory of communication where making meaning is derived from and across different modes, including language, film, images, gestures, messages, and more (Cohen & Cowen, 2011).

Parent library: The foundational library that creates a sense of place for families to access books and materials to check out and take home (Policastro, Mazeski & McTague, 2010–2011).

Phonemic awareness: The ability to manipulate the sounds in words orally (Tompkins, 2013).

Phonological awareness: An understanding that labels are made from bits of sound and that these bits can be reconfigured in many ways to construct new words and sounds (Seel, 2012).

Read-aloud: A classroom activity where the teacher reads a selection to the children. The selection can be fiction, nonfiction, or an informational text. The teacher might stop at specific points and ask the children questions before, during, and after the story (Policastro & McTague, 2015).

Reading and writing workshop: A designated time when students read self-selected books and use comprehension strategies to respond to these books in their journals. Students are encouraged to respond using higher-level thinking, not simply recalling and summarizing what happened (Kletzien, 1992).

Shared book reading: Also called "shared book experience," this method was invented by Holdaway (1979) as a way to recreate in the classroom the one-on-one reading experiences children have when they are read to by a parent. Children being read to at home can see the text; they interact with it as they point out what they notice and ask questions (Gill, 2006).

Summative assessment: Tests that are given at the end of a unit or lesson in formats that may include question/answer, multiple-choice, and fill-in-the-blank responses. Students typically receive a score from a summative assessment, and it is considered "high-stakes"(Policastro, McTague & Mazeski, 2016).

Vocabulary: The broad, all-purpose terms that appear across content areas but that may vary in meaning because of the subject itself (Bauman & Graves, 2010).

Living Literacy Forms for Home

Interest Tracker

Example: Today at the zoo, my child wanted to return to the giraffes. This is the third time that she asked to go to the zoo to see the giraffes.	**Example:** I noticed that my son is very interested in digger construction trucks. He stopped and watched a truck digging a hole in a nearby lot today.	**Example:** My son really loves putting together model airplanes and especially likes fighter jets and planes. He knows many details regarding the types as well.

Finding the Evidence Game

This game is for both fiction and nonfiction selections and makes use of the cards on pages 114–115.

Directions: This game board can be used with several players. Players can take turns moving along the game board each time they find the evidence.

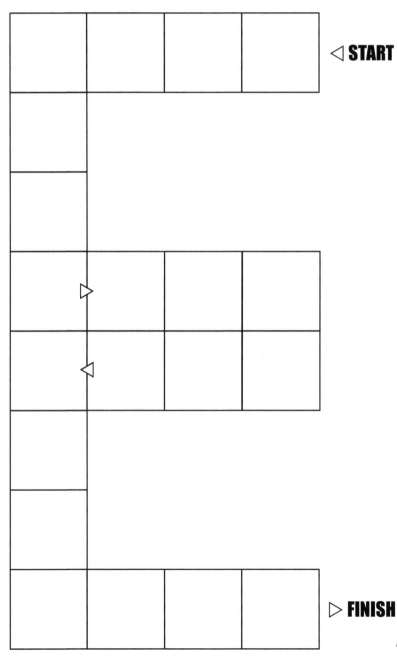

Fiction Cards

What is the name of the main character in the story? Find it in the book.	Where does the story take place? Find it in the book.
Name three things that happened in the story in sequence. Find the sequence in the book.	What challenges did the characters face in the story? Find them in the book.
How did the story conclude? Find the evidence to support your answer.	How did the characters solve their challenges? Find the evidence to support your answers.
Describe where the story takes place. Find the evidence to support your answer.	When does this story take place? Find the evidence to support your answer.

Nonfiction Cards

What is the main topic in this book? Find evidence to support your answer.	Find some information in the text that you think is easy to understand, and support your answer with evidence.
State at least two facts that are new to you, and find evidence to support them in the book.	Find some information that you think is difficult to understand, and support your answer with evidence.
What are some of the most important facts in this book and why? Find the evidence to support your answer.	What do you think the author's main point of view is for writing this informational text? Find evidence to support your answer.
Find two vocabulary words that are new to you, and find the definitions within the text.	If you had to persuade another person to read this book, what evidence from the text would you use?

Living Literacy
Family Outing Planner

Before the Outing

- Have fun planning the outing.
- Find brochures and other information to share before you set out.
- Do research on the outing as a family.

During the Outing

- Take photographs to document the experiences.
- Keep a journal, and write about the outing.

After the Outing

- Have conversations and talk about what you learned.
- What questions do we still have?
- What do we want to learn more about?
- Make a collage, create a scrapbook, or frame photos to document the experience.

Keeping Track of Our Reading: Documenting Family Literacy

Books Read Aloud	Books We Discussed

Books and Information Shared	Books We Want to Read

Back-to-school Planner

One Month Before School	One Week Before School
<ul><li>Have casual conversations about going to school.</li><li>Ask questions about feelings and excitement.</li><li>Get the list of school supplies, and begin checking off the list.</li><li>Let your child participate in and make choices about supplies.</li><li>Read books about the first day of school.</li></ul>	<ul><li>Continue conversations.</li><li>Continue to check off supply list.</li><li>Check out the school website.</li><li>Check the teacher's school website.</li><li>Visit the school if it is the first time attending.</li><li>Set bedtime schedules earlier.</li></ul>

One Day Before School	The First Days of School
• Get backpacks ready with supplies. • Start a journal with your child to document thoughts and feelings. • Read bedtime stories. • Get to bed early.	• Have lots of conversations centered on the school day. • Get into the homework routine right away. • Take photographs of the first days of school. • Do homework together.

Maupin House
capstone

At Maupin House by Capstone Professional, we continue to look for professional development resources that support grades K–8 classroom teachers in areas, such as these:

- Literacy
- Content-area Literacy
- Assessment
- Technology
- Standards-based Instruction
- Classroom Management

- Language Arts
- Research-based Practices
- Inquiry
- Differentiation
- School Safety
- School Community

If you have an idea for a professional development resource, visit our Become an Author website at: http://www.capstonepub.com/classroom/professional-development/become-an-author/

There are two ways to submit questions and proposals.

You may send them electronically to: proposals@capstonepd.com

You may send them via postal mail. Please be sure to include a self-addressed stamped envelope for us to return materials.

Acquisitions Editor
Capstone Professional
1 N. LaSalle Street, Suite 1800
Chicago, IL 60602